CW01499672

MUSH LOVE

MUSHROOM CULTIVATION: 21 STEP-BY-STEP METHODS TO BECOME THE COMPLETE HOME-GROWER IN AS LITTLE AS 4 WEEKS

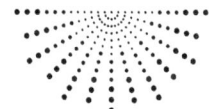

KRIS ROWSAN

CONTENTS

Before I start, I just want to quickly share a few fun facts about mushrooms.

- Trees were not always a part of our beloved planet. Before the trees, there were gigantic tree sized mushrooms that covered the earth.
- An edible wild mushroom called Laetiporus sulphureus has the taste and texture of fried chicken. Watch out for when it grows in Yew trees as this can cause it to consume toxins of the Yew tree, thus making them toxic to humans, so best to avoid them!
- A certain theory of evolution, The Stoned Ape theory, hypothesizes that the consumption of 'magic' mushrooms might have played a role in Homo Sapiens diverging from the less developed apes.
- Reindeer have been known to go out of their way to seek out hallucinogenic mushrooms. These mushrooms are thought to give reindeer a high similar to that of humans as they have been reported to act 'drunkenly' and aimlessly run around and make strange noises.
- In 2004, while studying breast cancer in women, it was deduced that a group of women

who consumed green tea and mushrooms, narrowed their risk of breast cancer by almost 90%.[1]

- It's often assumed that that mushrooms are more closely related to plants due their plant like appearance and static nature. However they are more closely related to humans. The Animal Kingdom diverged from the Fungi Kingdom 1.538 billion years ago.

Chicken of the Woods

INTRODUCTION

For more than half of my life, I was convinced that the largest living organism on planet earth was a blue whale. Around 10 years ago, I was proven wrong when I first heard of the 2400-year-old ginormous "honey mushroom" that covers an area of 2,200 acres (almost all of which extends roughly 3 feet underground, by the way). It is still growing and feeding off the nearby greens in its forest today, and at this point, it is considered the largest living being on the planet, weighing roughly the same as 4 blue whales. This honey mushroom, or *Armillaria ostoyae*, sits comfortably in the Malheur National Forest in Oregon, and is just one example of how vast and intriguing the world of mushrooms truly is.

Everyone knows that we can eat mushrooms, and when people do think of them, the white button mushrooms that we all see at our local supermarkets are likely what spring to mind. However, this is just one tiny facet of the fungi kingdom. Mushrooms play many roles in society that most people are likely not aware of. For example, did you know that fungus plays a role in modern medicine, such as penicillin the antibiotic? Are you aware that mushrooms can be used to make materials such as textiles, cleaning products, styrofoam-like packaging, and even biofuels? Mushrooms have an immensely diverse array of applications, and likely many more uses which are yet to even be discovered.

Outside of society, the complexity of the mushroom world doesn't cease to amaze. There is a mushroom in the wild, Ophiocordyceps unilateralis to be specific, that is a parasitic fungus. This fungus infects the brains of ants and upon seizing control of their minds, compels them to climb up the nearest plant as a vantage point where it will then completely colonize the insect and sprout a fruiting body which will release even more spores to infect new ants. On a slightly brighter note, there are also mushrooms in nature which glow in the dark.

As I've learned more and more about mushrooms over the years, I've only become increasingly fascinated. It all started while growing up on a homestead in the UK where my parents were avid gardeners. At the age of 16, they bought me my first mushroom growing kit, and so began my journey into the world of mushroom cultivation, and the kingdom of fungi. While I always felt that I was destined to be a gardener myself, I never imagined that it would lead me here, writing this book. With over 10 years of experience, after going through my own trials and tribulations, I am ecstatic that I now have the opportunity to share my bank of knowledge with all home growers. Whether your goal is to simply get started growing gourmet mushrooms or to expand your current cultivation knowledge, I hope that this book will be for you, the book I wish I had when I was first starting out.

When I began writing this book, the goal I was hoping to achieve was to put together an extensive resource with reliable step by step methods that home growers can replicate easily and successfully. That being said, there are 21 methods regarding growing mushrooms, making your own spawn, and other important techniques that can all be applied to make you a well-rounded grower. I hope that by the end of this book you will have the tools and the confidence to get your mushroom cultivation journey up and running within 4 weeks.

However, bear in mind as you read this book that there is no single correct way to grow mushrooms. Between a number of variables including experience, local climate, accessibility to certain materials, variety of mushroom, available space and time, lies the possibility for many different routes to the same destination. While I have tried to lay out numerous different options for people who might be in different situations, the key to becoming a successful mushroom cultivator is adapting and learning as you go, based on your personal circumstances. Use the beginner methods in this book to create a foundation for your growing knowledge, learn the basics thoroughly, and once you're comfortable, move on to the slightly more advanced techniques.

Lastly, like many endeavors in life, growing mushrooms might not necessarily be a smooth sailing journey, but don't let failures be a reason to give up. Trust me, I have made every mistake in the book. Learn from your mistakes and familiarize yourself with the unique set of conditions and processes that growing mushrooms requires, and apply that knowledge in your future grows. The most successful growers commit to this cycle of learning and applying, and if you do the same, you will obtain a skill set that can be used to feed your friends and family, or even accumulate enough mushrooms to sell at your local farmers' market–not many people can say they've done that!

Pursuing mushroom cultivation, initially as a hobby, ended up being one of the most gratifying ventures I've ever taken part in. I hope that this book instills in you the same sense of excitement that I've always had.

GET TO KNOW ME–I'M A FUNGI!

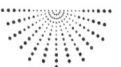

*W*hen deciding to take on mushroom cultivation, it's beneficial to learn as much as you can in order to better understand the process as a whole, and in turn, become a more effective grower. In this chapter we'll learn a little bit about fungi and applications of mushrooms in society, followed by some basic biology and the life cycle of the mushroom.

FUNGI IN A NUTSHELL

The word 'fungus,' or plural fungi, is the latin word for mushroom. Of course, the edible mushrooms that we are most familiar with are indeed fungi, but the term also encompasses numerous other types of fungi including yeasts, molds, mildews, and rusts. While there are over 140,000 known types of species, scientists estimate the actual number of fungal species to be well over one million, however, there is no conclusive number.

Fungi play an essential role in balancing our ecosystems, and exist within almost every habitat, thriving in moist and dark environments, feeding off of dead or decaying materials. Some even do well in seemingly harsh conditions like the tundra living symbiotically with surrounding plants, while others form parasitic relationships with insects or crops. However, fungi (and also bacteria) are responsible for the breakdown of organic matter which releases oxygen, carbon, nitrogen and phosphorus back into the environment and atmosphere. Without them, this organic matter would otherwise not be recycled and food chains would render incomplete.

There was a point in the past where fungi were included in the plant kingdom, but when they were found to differ by lack of chlorophyll and chloroplasts, they were separated into two distinct kingdoms. Similar to plant cells, fungi are encompassed by a robust cell wall, but the cell walls of fungi are made up of chitin (which is also found in the exoskeleton of insects) and glucan. Plant cell walls, on the other hand, are made up of cellulose.

Similar to animals, however, fungi are heterotrophs and they must obtain their nutrition from their diets.

Their mycelial networks secrete digestive enzymes that break down the surrounding organic matter, allowing the fungi to easily ingest the nutrients and release what they don't need back into the ecosystem.

Generally, the visible part of any fungus is called a sporophore (or fruiting body) and these sporophores can present in an extensive array of shapes, sizes, and colors. While some are too small to see with the naked eye, others, such as the umbrella-shaped stem and cap we all know and love, are always on display. Although mushrooms are not the most abundant of the fungi, they are the most easily identified.

The fruiting body that is a mature mushroom consists of the stem, a cap, gills, a volva, mycelium, and spores. In short, mycelial networks grow and expand underground, and when enough mycelium has formed, certain points will condense and a fruiting body will extend outwards. Once mature, the fruiting body releases spores, which upon finding a suitable environment, will initiate further mycelial growth, and the process begins again. This will be covered in more detail later in this chapter, but for now, let's talk about our relationship to mushrooms as a society!

MUSHROOMS IN SOCIETY

As stated earlier, mushrooms are present in society in numerous forms. A primary role of mushrooms, as you probably have already guessed, is as a crop that can be cultivated, and this of course is the main focus of this book. However, there's no harm in discovering the multitude of other uses that mushrooms have to get you excited about the world of fungi!

Most obviously, mushrooms are a part of cuisines all over the world. It's common to see button mushrooms and portobellos at your local supermarket, but other commonly eaten mushrooms are shiitake, lion's mane, maitake, oysters, enoki, and wine caps, which are also commonly cultivated. Morels and chanterelles are another two types of mushrooms which are often eaten, but are generally foraged as opposed to grown at home. Some fungi are also used as fermentation agents with grains and fruits to create beer and wines. Additionally, yeast is a fungi used when making breads and other baked items.

Mushrooms are also found to have numerous health benefits. As time passes, scientists, nutritionists, doctors, and other health professionals continue to present to the public the different benefits that varying species of mushrooms can provide for many different illnesses. For example, the Turkey Tail has been rendered down as a tea in order to extract the beta-glucans which are present, for a few hundred years. These abundant beta-glucans pack an immune punch, and have displayed anti-cancerous properties.[1] Reishi have also been found to have immune boosting properties as well as combating fatigue and depression.[2] To add one more to the list, Lion's Mane mushrooms contain compounds that help promote the growth of neural cells, improve cognition, and protect against dementia.[3]

Moving on, there are mushrooms that present hallucinogenic properties, and you can't write a book about mushrooms without at least mentioning these. Hallucinogenic mushrooms contain an active compound called psilocybin, and regardless of the fact that they are illegal in the UK and most US states, they still exist as part of society. However, although these hallucinogenic mushrooms do exist, they are a very small facet of extant mushroom species, and this book is not a guide for the cultivation of such active species. The focus of this book will remain on gourmet mushrooms which can be grown at home for food.

Lastly, mushrooms play a large role in the research of environmental bioremediation. Bioremediation is the use of microorganisms in breaking down toxic pollutants. While mushrooms are known for breaking down organic matter, there have also been studies which have shown they are capable of breaking down inorganic matter. A huge problem that the world is currently facing is the pollution of clean soil, water, and air, as a result of mass industrialization. Although still a relatively new area of research, mushrooms have shown some promising results in their ability to bioremediate agricultural wastes, heavy metals, and toxic organic wastes.[4]

By now, I'm sure you can see that mushrooms can benefit society in many different ways. With less than 10 percent of the fungi world known to humans, it's incredible to think about the potential applications of these organisms as we learn more about them.

THE LIFE CYCLE OF A MUSHROOM

Before we get into the nitty gritty of mushroom growing, let's go over the growth of mushrooms in their life cycle. This will help you later on in understanding which phase your mushrooms are at.

When thinking of mushrooms, the image that comes to mind for many of those who are new to growing, is that of a stem and a cap that appear to be growing out of the ground, often seen walking through forested areas, or in a garden. However, this stem and cap tell not even close to half of the story. The fruiting bodies we see are the very end stage of the mushroom life cycle, and to get there, large amounts of growth and activity will have gone on before these actually appear. So how does this happen?

Dispersal of Spores

Although not literally fruit, we call mushrooms the "fruiting bodies" of the fungi. These fruiting bodies begin their life cycle as what is called a "spore." Millions of microscopic spores that work in a similar way as "seeds" (but are not actually seeds) are located below the mushroom's "umbrella" or "cap." A single mushroom has the capacity of producing billions of spores throughout its lifetime which travel with the wind away from the parent body, but only a small number of these will actually land where they can germinate. When these spores do align with some sort of growth medium (or substrate) like logs or compost, the spores will then begin to germinate.

Spore Germination

When spores land in an area with favorable conditions and a suitable substrate, very fine fungal filaments, known as hyphae, will begin extending out from the spores. These hyphae eventually cluster with other hyphae from compatible spores that are nearby. When these compatible hyphae meet and combine in their growth, we get what is known as fertile mycelium.

Mycelium

Mycelium, as discussed earlier, is a lot like the roots of a plant that absorb nutrients from its surroundings. A developing network of mycelium appears as a web-like structure that is capable of providing necessary elements for the production of mushrooms, by breaking down surrounding organic matter. Mycelium at this stage will expand at an exponential rate, and will repel its competitors through a multitude of protective enzymes that act as an immune system.

Hyphal Knots and Primordia

While growing mushrooms, this is the stage where you get to see the mushroom finally popping up and creating shape. Once the mycelium has developed enough, certain areas will become very dense, resulting in what is known as hyphal knots. A hyphal knot is a place where the pinhead (or primordia) will sprout from. Baby mushrooms are termed pinheads, and this transformation of hyphal knots into baby mushrooms is a fascinating process that can be witnessed directly while growing mushrooms.

Mature Fruiting Bodies

Once you know what a baby mushroom looks like, it's not difficult to spot one. One might think that all the pins from the mycelial network will grow into big beautiful mushrooms, but that is not the case! Many of the pins will stop growing after reaching a certain form, and the mycelium will focus its energy on the most promising pinheads to grow into mature fruit bodies. Once the fruiting bodies have fully matured, they will then release their own spores, and thus, the life cycle begins again!

Now that you have a brief understanding of the life-cycle of a mushroom, it's time to move on to how these stages apply when actually cultivating mushrooms! But first, in the next section I've provided a list of common terms you'll hear throughout the remainder of the book.

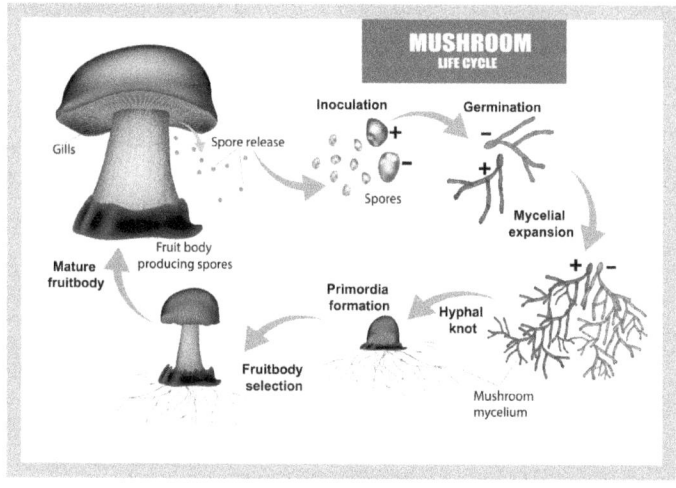

Life cycle of a mushroom illustration

Glossary of Mushroom Terminology

If you are new to growing mushrooms, you will likely hear a lot of words that will sound quite foreign to you. Below is a list of these common terms and phrases that will be seen throughout the book. Many will be explained in greater detail as we go on.

· · ·

Agar: A jelly-like substance which is used in petri dishes to grow mycelium culture. It provides a very nutritious food supply for the mycelium

Autoclave/Pressure Cooker/Pressure Canner: A large pot that can be pressurized with steam. It can be used for sterilizing grains and other substrates.

Bulk substrate: Similar to a block substrate but can be any type of substrate; sawdust, coco coir, straw etc.

Colonization: The process in which the mycelium grows through a substrate, a grain or an petri dish filled with agar. Once the mycelium has fully worked its way through the whole of the substrate it is said to be fully colonized.

Contamination: Typically bacteria or any other unwanted fungi living on either your mushrooms, fruiting blocks or agar plates.

Culture: A piece of living mushroom mycelium that has the genetics and DNA to produce fruiting bodies

Fruiting Block: This is a cube-shaped block of supplemented sawdust that has been fully colonized with mycelium. This will give rise to your mushrooms.

Fruiting Body: The part of the mushroom we can actually eat which is the stem and the cap. What most people consider to be a 'Mushroom'

Fruiting: The stage at which the white mycelium on the substrate turns into the fruiting body of the mushroom.

Gypsum: This is calcium sulfate and is used as a supplement to enhance the nutritional value of it to your mycelium. (*This is optional)

Inoculation: The process of adding a living mycelium culture to a grain/sawdust jar to make spawn, or the process of adding spawn to a bulk substrate to give rise to mushrooms.

Laminar Flow Hood: A high tech piece of equipment that you can carry out sterile practices in front of. It allows for a constant circulation of clean air which is needed for some techniques. (*Not essential for small-scale home growers–a still air box (SAB) will do the trick).

Pasteurization: The process in which your bulk substrate is heated to kill many of the competing microorganisms which gives your mycelium the best chance at succeeding in colonizing the substrate.

Shotgun Fruiting Chamber: A container with many holes drilled throughout all sides. It provides more optimal conditions for your mushrooms.

Still Air Box (SAB): A low tech piece of equipment used to provide a more sterile working environment than working in the open air.

Spawn: Any material (usually sawdust or grain) that has been colonized by the mycelium which can then be used to inoculate a fruiting substrate

Spores: Sometimes referred to as the 'seeds' of the mushrooms. They are usually kept on the underside of the mushroom caps and are released in order to allow the mushroom to reproduce

Sterilization: The process in which the substrate or grain is heated to higher temperatures then pasteurization and for a longer period to completely kill off all micro-organisms.

Substrate: A growing medium for mycelium. This can be cardboard, straw, Coco coir, sawdust, manure, compost or grains.

THE CULTIVATION STATION: UNDERSTANDING THE CULTIVATION PROCESS

I have vivid memories from growing up on a large homestead with my mom and dad, where a lot of the time they were outside tending to their impressive vegetable patch, cleaning it out and always making improvements. However, one agricultural activity they didn't participate in was that of growing gourmet mushrooms. I still remember my mom once telling me she didn't think it was worth the time or effort to grow mushrooms. One thing that is common between home gardeners is their love for growing fruiting plants such as tomatoes or potatoes. But we rarely see or hear about people growing mushrooms at home, and this might be due to the misconception that growing mushrooms is extremely difficult.

Although it can seem overwhelming at first, growing mushrooms can become quite easy once you get the

hang of it. Yes, it does have a unique set of requirements, but once these are learned, great rewards lie
ahead! You just have to remain consistent and be
willing to learn and improve your technique with each
new grow. Now let's get into the cultivation process
itself, so you know what to expect when you start.

GROWTH OF MUSHROOMS IN THE WILD

We have already spoken about the life cycle of a mushroom, but let's recap quickly before moving on. In
nature, mature mushrooms release spores from the
gills under their caps, and the spores are dispersed
throughout the area via wind or air movement. Once
in favorable conditions and a suitable growing medium
(otherwise known as a substrate), spores begin to
germinate and produce filamentous bodies called
hyphae. For every viable spore that comes into contact
with a suitable surface, new hyphae will be produced.
Subsequently, upon finding compatibility, two hyphae
will exchange genetic material amongst each other
after joining, creating the mycelium.

At this stage, this hyphal growth accelerates producing
the immense mycelial network that absorbs nutrients
from its surroundings. Once the mycelium successfully
colonizes its substrate and has accumulated enough
nutrients to fruit, it condenses and winds around itself
into hyphal knots from which it starts pushing

pinheads (or primordia) up to the surface. These are tiny structures that look more like little mushroom caps, some of which will then grow into mature mushrooms. The mature mushrooms will then release their own spores, and the cycle starts again.

THE MUSHROOM CULTIVATION PROCESS

By now you have a clear idea of how a basic mushroom grows in the wild. The reason for getting you accustomed to this process is to quite simply understand the life cycle, as without this foundational knowledge, the steps for cultivating mushrooms can become quite confusing. Whatever route you go down, whether that be to solely grow at home or even growing on a commercial scale, the methods for the cultivation process will follow the same basic principles which stem from the life cycle of mushrooms in the wild.

CREATING A STERILE ENVIRONMENT

If you have any prior knowledge on growing mushrooms, then you most likely have heard of the phrase "sterile environment." If not, that's fine; we're going to cover all of that now. The first unofficial step to cultivating mushrooms is creating a sterile environment. Is a sterile environment as important as everyone seems to think? Yes, it is. Creating a sterile environment is essential when growing mushrooms, as it allows the best chance for your desired mushroom to succeed and triumph over the competition of other contaminants like mold or other fungi.

A valid question that people often ask is: "Why do I have to be so careful with sterilization when mushrooms grow in the wild where nothing is sterile?" The answer to this is that in the wild, mushrooms are not forced to grow at a certain location or under certain conditions like they are when we try to grow mushrooms at home. In nature, mushrooms grow in a much more balanced process within their ecosystem. While they of course still have to compete with other microorganisms, we wouldn't necessarily notice when mushrooms fail to thrive in nature, in the same way we would notice it during our own coerced growing attempts. Simply put, sterile environments and clean practice reduce the potential number of competing microorganisms, and there are several ways to achieve this.

When growing mushrooms indoors, if possible, choose one room to grow in–this will now be your growing room. It is important that this room is thoroughly cleaned prior to any growing attempt and in an ideal world, to be kept clean all the time. However, I do understand that those of you living in small apartments might not have a spare room to utilize as your mushroom growing room. Not to worry, you are still able to grow in any room that you use regularly, but you will just need to make sure you give it a really good clean beforehand. When I moved into my London apartment I had to ditch the high tech gear and go back to very small scale, low-tech methods–it is possible, and trust me, it can be achieved by anyone in most living conditions.

Although creating a sterile environment isn't rocket science, it can require a bit of effort, but don't stress too much about this–I have made that mistake before. Before you start, choose where you want to carry out the process. Mop or thoroughly clean the floor of the room you choose, preferably with antibacterial cleaning solution, or a diluted bleach solution. A word of caution, I would avoid growing in carpeted rooms as carpets and rugs are a perfect trap for many more contaminants as compared to hard flooring. If you are now sitting there thinking, "my house is fully carpeted" or "I have rugs throughout my house," again, please don't panic. I have carried out the inoculation process in a carpeted room a few times and still managed to get a good crop, and others before you have done it too. To reduce the chance of contamination in carpeted areas, it's a good idea to vacuum regularly, but not immediately before working with your mushrooms as it can stir up contaminants into the air. You can also potentially have your carpets deep-cleaned or shampooed sometime prior to starting the process. Growing in a carpeted room is not ideal, but my point is that it can definitely still be done.

Keep your refrigerators clean and regularly dispose of any leftover foods and garbage, as these can be hotspots for troublesome microorganisms like mould. If you have an air conditioner unit or any fans in your mushroom growing room, then give these a good clean too.

It also goes without saying that the surface you choose to use will also need to be thoroughly cleaned. Always initially wipe the surfaces down with water to get off any obvious dirt, food, or grease, and then spray a good anti-bacterial spray or a 7:1 solution of water and isopropyl alcohol, and let it sit for 5 or so minutes to let it take effect. Then, with a fresh kitchen paper towel, fully wipe down the surface. Do not use a dirty kitchen rag or any other previously used cleaning items, as these will obviously be hot spots for contaminants.

When possible, take a shower before starting, especially if you have been out doing any sort of physical activity or work. While I wouldn't say this step is essential, it can't hurt! What is essential though, is that you thoroughly clean your hands and forearms with warm, soapy water for a good 30 seconds to really make sure they're clean before starting. Air purifiers can also make life easier by filtering out the air and give you a relatively cleaner atmosphere. Once you've created a sterile environment, you're ready to move on!

5 STAGES OF MUSHROOM CULTIVATION

Stage 1: Choosing and Obtaining Mushroom Spawn

We have already discussed spores in detail and know that they work like seeds for the growth of mushrooms, but what is mushroom spawn? Spawn is any material or substrate that has already been fully colonized by a mycelial network. The mycelial network that grows underground in the wild is essentially what the spawn is mimicking.

There are several different types of spawn that are made using different substrates depending on which type of mushroom you are trying to grow. For example, a common type of spawn is grain spawn which can be made using brown rice grains, rye grains, or barley, among others. Sawdust is also used to create spawn, and plug spawn are available for growing on logs outdoors. These will be covered in much more detail in Chapter 4.

So, why do we use spawn? Using premade spawn can be a much easier and quicker way of beginning the cultivation process. Making your own spawn can be a bit daunting at first, and requires a more sterile environment, which is why it is recommended at least when starting out, to purchase premade spawn. This can be done either online or at a store from a variety of producers. You'll just have to take the time to find a good source, and these may vary depending on where you live.

Again, you can produce your own spawn–it's not impossible, but it does require a bit more effort as well as more sterile procedures. If you're keen on doing so, I've provided instructions for a low-tech method of making your own spawn in Chapter 5! Once you've either obtained or made your own spawn, the next step is inoculation.

Stage 2: Inoculation

This step is where creating and maintaining a sterile environment comes into play. When you receive your premade spawn, it will be in sterile packaging, and if you've made it yourself, it should be in sterile jars. You want to ensure that you're inoculating your spawn into a sterile substrate, in a sterile environment. Again, this is just to prevent competing microorganisms which will give your mushroom spawn the best chance for growth and colonization of the substrate.

There are two things you can do once you have your hands on some mushroom spawn. You can either inoculate more grain/sawdust/etc. with your current spawn to create even more spawn, or you can inoculate the spawn into a bulk (or fruiting) substrate where the mushrooms will eventually grow. Inoculating simply means introducing the spawn into a substrate (or growing medium), and substrates will differ depending on your chosen type of mushroom. This will be covered in greater detail in Chapter 4.

Stage 3: Incubation

Inoculation is followed by incubation. This stage will require a bit of patience, as you want to allow enough time for the mycelium to fully colonize the substrate. You'll need to place the substrate in an environment that is warm (mushrooms colonize best at temperatures between 70-75°F) and dark, with minimal sunlight. You want to avoid temperatures exceeding 80°F because this will increase the chances of survival for any competing microorganisms. Light exposure is a hotly contested subject among mushroom cultivators in regards to how much light mushrooms should receive during incubation. Some argue that they should be left to colonise in a room or cupboard with absolutely no light, and others say that indirect sunlight is important at this stage to help with the mushrooms' circadian rhythms. In my opinion, it doesn't matter too much what approach you go for. Personally, I colonise my fruiting blocks in a room with minimal indirect sunlight but I have gotten equally great flushes when I have left them in a dark cupboard.

You need to allow the mycelium to colonise for somewhere around a few weeks to a few months, depending on the type of mushroom. During this time your mycelium will be working hard to absorb all the nutrients from the substrate, and will start colonizing. By the end of it, you should have a relatively solid white block of mycelium! It's also important to keep in mind that the incubation stage is where you will most likely come across contamination if there is any, so be aware of the colors that will be mentioned in the contamination section later in this chapter.

Stage 4: Fruiting

Much like the name suggests, the substrate is then placed into certain fruiting conditions after the incubation period. You can start by cutting open the bag or opening the container that the substrate was placed in and exposing them to fresh air. At this point, the substrate is kept moist with water all through the day. You will see pinheads (primordia) forming on your substrate after a few days. These pinheads will grow to become mature mushrooms. Again this will be covered in greater detail in Chapter 4.

. . .

Stage 5: Harvesting

Mushrooms have varying harvesting periods depending on their type. As discussed earlier, just like mushrooms require different conditions for their growth depending on the species, similarly, the harvesting period is also dependent on the type of mushroom. A few types of mushrooms can be harvested and will regrow several times, and each new sprouting of mushroom is known as a flush. However, once the substrate loses all its nutrition, the mycelium ability to produce new flushes stops, which is also known as senescence.

CULTURE CONTAMINATION

Now that we've gone through the cultivation process and highlighted the importance of a sterile environment, we cannot ignore certain possibilities of culture contamination. Unfortunately, even when you take every measure to prevent contamination, it can still occur, because the favorable conditions we attempt to create for our mushrooms tend to be the same conditions that other microorganisms thrive in. Contamination is easily one of the biggest reasons that people give up on growing mushrooms. It can be extremely discouraging to spend hours on end cleaning and inoculating, or weeks to months waiting for your mycelium to grow, only to have to throw out a batch because of contaminants. That being said, it's best to be aware of the potential contaminants you might encounter.

Sticking to a basic definition of the word, contamination is simply anything that is living on your mushrooms, mycelium, or fruiting blocks, that isn't supposed to be there. Having said that, these contaminants are easy to identify and that certainly makes life easier. Mushroom mycelium is completely white and any spots on it or any kind of intruding element will usually be easily noticeable on it. Contaminants can be roughly classified into one of three groups; mold (fungi), bacteria, or pests. To avoid pests, simply ensure that you are keeping a clean workspace that won't attract insects or other bugs.

How can I identify contamination?

In my early days, there was nothing more frustrating to me than checking on my cultures and my mycelium and finding contamination. It truly made me realize the importance of learning how to identify the earliest indications of contaminants and how to deal with them accordingly. Don't lose hope–just because one of the cultures has gone bad, doesn't mean that the entire project has to go down.

One of the most obvious signs of contamination is discolored mycelium. Several species of molds boast bright colors. If you see a green, blue, grey or even black patch on or inside your grain jars, growing bags, or fruiting container, the culture has most likely already been contaminated. However, that being said, you need to be mindful of two colors; blue and yellow. If the mycelium turns blue, it might mean that your mycelium is bruised. If it is bruised, and not contaminated, it should turn back to a healthy white color in a matter of a couple to a few days. If the blue coloring has surpassed this time frame, you can most likely rule out bruising and confirm contamination. On the other hand, if mycelium turns light yellow or a light brown, it just means that the mycelium is aging and working up its defences against different kinds of bacteria.

Now alongside fungi, bacteria is also one of the causes of substrate contamination. Molds are easy to identify but with the bacteria, the situation becomes sticky–literally. Bacterial presence is identified through the production of slimy substances. These slimy patches will be visible on your grain or mycelium, indicating the excess production of moisture and can signify bacterial intrusion. Simultaneously, yellowish-brown stains will also appear and you may see a gel-like or crusty texture. This can be differentiated from aging mycelium because of this slimy, wet texture.

During the incubation phase, a healthy mycelium grows uniformly through any grain or substrate. Eventually, the hyphae will spread in all different directions but will converge within the growing medium. If you notice any partitioning or division among the hyphae, it might mean that there is some contamination inside your substrate that's not visible to you. At this point you can wait until you are out of the incubation period for your variety of mushroom to decide whether or not you need to start fresh.

You must closely monitor your culture at all times because a few fungal species are difficult to spot, and might not be visible to you. Their appearance can be deceptive and you may notice the difference once inspected closely. They have a bubble structured tip and look a lot like small hairy formations.

When I say that you have to monitor your culture it means that you might need to use a magnifying glass too. There are times when the texture of your culture or mycelium might look a bit dusty or you might notice a powdery substance sitting on top of your mycelium. Both of these conditions are easily identifiable under a magnifying glass and can be dealt with accordingly.

Upon finding contamination, throwing out the contaminated fruiting block or culture will be your best bet. If you try to open them to remove the infected part of the production, it will only create a bigger risk to your sterile environment.

. . .

Commonly Found Examples of Contamination

Here are a few types of contaminations that are commonly found in mushroom cultures.

Wet Spot

These can be easily found in grain spawn jars. Despite sterilization, the bacillus (the bacteria that causes wet spot) can at times survive in the form of endospores that are heat resistant. You will notice a dull grey slime forming inside the medium that is completely contaminated with the bacillus. It gives off a foul stench and the grain will look excessively drenched or wet, which is why it is called wet spot.

Bacterial Blotch

Bacterial blotches generally occur in the form of yellow or brown lesions around or next to the mushroom caps. The bacteria disperse with airborne soil grains and will contaminate your mushrooms if they are still wet after 4-6 hours of being watered. You can control this by bringing the humidity down and applying a chlorinated spray solution with 150 ppm chlorine.

Cobweb Mold

You would know that your culture is contaminated with this mold once you see a cotton-like substance covering your culture causing the mycelium to rot. The colour of this mold is relatively darker than the mycelium and the color difference will be noticeable. However, another way to tell it's a cobweb mold is the speed at which it spreads. It usually only takes 1 to 2 days to completely cover the whole casing, which is much faster than mycelial growth. You can reduce the risk of this contamination by bringing the humidity levels down and increasing the air circulation.

Green Mold

Green mold is identified by small spores that are green in color. Initially, this mold will envelop the whole container with a white rapidly spreading mycelium that will cause the mushrooms to rot and will produce greenish spores. This is generally a result of poor sanitation and flies and strictly following a sanitation routine will help you avoid this problem.

Red Bread Mold

This fungus is also called Neurospora, and it is generally present everywhere in nature but can commonly present in grain and agar when growing mushrooms. It's growth is very aggressive and can transfer from culture to culture even if your containers/jars are closed. If you're unfortunate enough to encounter this, I would recommend immediately getting rid of the contaminated cultures and re-sterilzing your working environment including all equipment.

Blue/Green Mold

This type of mold is also known as penicillium and is a common form of contamination for mushrooms cultivators. It's one of the easier signs of contamination to spot due to its color. These spores are also floating throughout the air constantly which makes them a more common problem than other types of contamination.

3

MUSHROOMS THAT CAN BE GROWN AT HOME

*B*y now I hope you have a good understanding of the basics of mushrooms. I know there is a lot of information and terminology to get to grips with, but slowly, it will all start to make sense! Let's get started with the fun stuff now and go through how we can best get growing gourmet mushrooms if you are a complete beginner.

The first, and by far the easiest method for growing, especially for a newbie, is using a growing kit. These ready-made kits include a fruiting block of the mushroom variety of your choice. The fruiting block is essentially a substrate which has already been fully colonized by a mycelial network that is ready to fruit when exposed to the right conditions. These kits serve as a learning model for beginners because you don't have to concern yourself with sterile methods of production, development of a growing room, or producing and maintaining cultures. They are also a great way to dip your toes into the world of mushroom cultivation without fully committing to the hobby. In the next chapter, I'll go over how to set up growing kits to get optimal yields from your fruiting block.

However, if you're past the grow-kit stage, or you just want to dive head first into growing, the following mushrooms are recommended. The following list includes quite a few different mushroom species that are often successfully grown at home, and the methods for these have been tested many times.

COMMONLY GROWN MUSHROOMS

Many different types of mushrooms can be grown at home. In this section, I'll cover some of the most commonly grown mushrooms, their cultivation difficulty, descriptions, and where they are found in nature.

MAITAKE (Grifola frondosa)

Often referred to as "dancing mushrooms" or "Hen of the Woods," Maitake mushrooms are delicious to eat and have a delicate texture. Maitake mushrooms present both nutritional and medicinal purposes, and it's no wonder it is one of the most commonly cultivated species. Although they are a bit on the challenging side of the grow-scale, they are worth it.

Description: Maitake present themselves with large, soft and fleshy bodies. In their initial stages of growth, the color can vary from greyish brown to grey as they grow older, with some even fading to a light yellow. The fruiting body caps look like layered flower petals, or layered hen feathers, hence the nickname, Hen of the Woods. These overlapping caps are roughly 1-5 inches in diameter and extend from the branching stems that are all attached to a single base.

Distribution and habitat: These mushrooms are native to northern deciduous forests with temperate weather. They are found mainly in North America, but can also be found in Japan. Maitake, fruit from the base of trees, particularly dead or dying hardwood trees, as they are a good source of nutrition for them.

Guidelines for growth: Maitake grows during the fall season. The spawning substrates that can be used for growing maitake are grains such as rye, brown rice, birdseed. Sawdust can be used for spawn as well. It is best to use large spawning bags or jars for spawning, and polypropylene bags or containers for fruiting. The spawning incubation temperature should be 70-75 °F or 20-24 °C. Fruiting substrates include wood-based mediums such as sawdust and wood chips for indoors, and for outdoors, hardwood logs can be used. Hardwood is best, and specifically oak wood, tends to yield the best results. Fruiting temperature should range from 50-70 °F. Fruiting generally starts from 4-6 weeks after inoculation and it takes another 4-6 weeks for the fronds to develop. You should try to maintain humidity levels somewhere between 75% to 85%

Wild Maitake mushroom

SHIITAKE (Lentinula edodes)

Common in Asian cultures for centuries, especially that of China, Japan, and Korea, Shiitake mushrooms are the second most cultivated species at home, and it's quite obvious why. They provide cuisines with a meaty and firm texture and a pleasant earthy aroma and taste. Not to mention, they are one of the easier mushrooms to grow. In Asian culture, they are grown on logs, and while some attempt to do this in North America, it has not fully caught on and is cultivated on large scales indoors instead.

Description: An ordinary shitake has a cap ranging from 2-8 inches in width. While growing, the cap is shaped like a dome, and eventually levels out to a more flat shape. The cap is generally dark brown and sometimes black initially, but as it matures it gradually fades to a light brown. The gills are white, but will turn a brownish color if damaged.

Shiitake growing on logs

Distribution and habitat: The Shiitake mushroom is native to Korea, China, and Japan, and some regions of Southeast Asia as well. Shiitake is known to grow on dead or decaying tree trunks, mainly the Shii tree or other Asian oaks and beeches.

Guidelines for growth: If growing outdoors on logs, Shiitake will fruit in the fall. However, with sawdust bags, they can be grown year round indoors. Spawning substrates commonly used for this mushroom are grains (rye, birdseed, brown rice) and hardwood sawdust. You can also obtain plug/dowel spawn for Shiitake to grow them on logs. The spawning incubation temperature should range from 21-27 °C or 70-80 °F. Fruiting substrates for this mushroom are obtained from mainly wooden sources such as sawdust blocks, or hardwood logs. The fruiting temperature should be around 60-70 °F or 16-21 °C. It takes about 4-8 weeks for the spawn to fruit starting from the time of inoculation into the bulk substrate. The humidity should be maintained around 70-80%

LION'S MANE (Hericium erinaceus)

Lion's mane is famous for its extraordinary lobster-esque flavor, unique crab-like texture, and its unusual hair-like appearance. Also known as "Pom Pom" mushrooms and "Old Man's Beard," in the mushroom world they are unlike any other mushroom, with their majestic willow-like display. Lion's Mane is often used as a substitute for meat, but mainly for seafood. There is also research that shows this type of mushroom to have dementia-fighting as well as anti-inflammatory properties. Lion's Mane is quite delicate and can easily bruise, which makes it a hard sell for grocery stores. However, because it can be easily cultivated at home, it's the perfect choice for home-growers who know they likely can't get it anywhere else, but still want to enjoy it.

Description: Lion's mane is composed of dangling white strands that cascade downward. They are white colored from the very beginning of their fruiting stage up until their most mature stages in which they will sometimes turn a light yellow color.

Lion's Mane growing on a log in the wild

Distribution and habitat: Mostly found in the southern parts of the US, Lion's mane is also found throughout North America, China, Europe, and Japan. Lion's mane feeds on dead or decaying oak, maple, walnut, or other trees with broad leaves. In the wild, you will find them growing on logs or tree stumps.

Growth parameters: Lion's Mane season is late summer into fall if growing outdoors. The spawning substrate used for this mushroom is grains such as rye, millet, birdseed, or popcorn. Hardwood sawdust is also used as a spawning substrate, as well as plug/dowel spawn. For growing spawn, containers such as jars, or spawning bags are used. The spawn incubation temperature should be around 70-75 °F or 21-24 °C. Fruiting substrate should be hardwood-based, such as sawdust blocks supplemented with wheat bran, or straw for indoor growing. For outdoor cultivation, hardwood logs can be used. Fruiting temperature should be around 65-75 °F or 18-24 °C. Lion's Mane will begin to fruit after roughly 2-4 weeks of incubation. Humidity for optimal growth should be around 90%.

OYSTER (Pleurotus ostreatus)

Oyster mushrooms are by far the easiest and quickest mushroom to grow. There are many different species of oyster including the King Oyster, Pearl Oyster, and the different strains which come in varying colors including blue, grey, yellow, and even pink! Oysters are known for their tenacious mycelium's ability to fight off other competitors as well as their lack of pickiness with substrates. These take the cake when it comes to the number of different substrates they can be grown on which include straw, sawdust, coffee grounds, compost, wood chips, on logs, and even cardboard or toilet paper. Oyster mushrooms have several health benefits such as immunity improvement, strength regulation, and anti-cancerous properties. With their high success rates and high yields, in addition to their variety of strain, oysters are a popular choice for beginner growers.

Description: Oyster mushrooms are most commonly brown, grey, or white, however as stated above, can be many different colors depending on the species. These slightly differ from the average mushroom with a cap that is connected laterally to the stem, as opposed to centrally.

Oyster mushrooms growing out of straw

Distribution and habitat: Oyster mushrooms are found in North America, across Europe, and in some regions of Asia, depending on the species. They can be found on hardwood trees.

Guidelines for growth: Oyster mushrooms boast aggressive growth and can grow all year round. Spawning substrates for oyster mushrooms range from grains to sawdust. Oyster mushrooms can be spawned in containers or jars and the incubation temperature should be roughly 75 °F. The fruiting substrates for oyster mushrooms are most commonly straw, and sometimes sawdust. However, Oysters are known to be aggressive and have the ability to grow on many other mediums as mentioned above. The fruiting temperature should be around 65-70°F. Oysters begin fruit after 2-3 weeks of inoculation. These mushrooms require 90-95% humidity levels for optimal growth.

BUTTON MUSHROOMS & PORTOBELLOS (Agaricus bisporus)

Button mushrooms are extremely common, and the type of mushroom you likely see all the time at your local grocery store. These are definitely a mushroom to try out as a beginner because they are really easy to grow, and they fruit in large numbers. They can be cultivated both indoors and outdoors. There are white and brown button mushrooms, and brown button mushrooms are the baby version of portobellos, which are discussed next–the same growth parameters can be applied regardless of whether you want to grow button mushrooms, or allow them to fully develop into portobellos.

Portobello mushrooms are big in size and have a flat, rounded cap that can grow up to six inches in diameter. Portobellos are also known as Portabella mushrooms, due to a slight change in the name, both of which names were part of a marketing ploy in the 80's. Again, these are actually just large, brown button mushrooms, and in their smaller form they are also known as Crimini mushrooms, or just baby portobellos. Portobellos (or buttons) are one of the easiest types of mushrooms to cultivate, and generally provide high yields.

Description: Portobellos have a thick fleshy cap, that is light to dark brown on top, but white within. These take the shape of a dome initially, and flatten out with age. Button mushrooms are essentially just the Portobellos before they have reached full development. These mushrooms have a centralized fibrous, short stem. The gills on the underside are dark brown to black.

Distribution and habitat: These mushrooms are commonly found throughout the temperate regions of Europe and North America. Portobello mushrooms are predominantly found in grounds abundant with organic matter, or nutrient rich soil.

Guidelines for growth: If growing outdoors, Portobellos will do well in milder temperatures from 50-70 °F. Indoors, they can be grown year round. Spawning takes roughly 3 weeks, and temperatures should remain around 70-75 °F during the incubation period. Substrates for spawning are typically grain spawns, and spawning can be done in polypropylene bags, or jars. Fruiting substrates include compost, manure, or compost- or manure-enriched straw. Containers or trays that are around 12 inches in depth work best for fruiting. It takes around 3-4 weeks for portobellos to fully develop, but they can be harvested at whatever size you prefer. Temperatures should be around 65 °F for the fruiting period, with 90% humidity.

Button mushrooms

ENOKI (Flammulina velutipes)

Enoki mushrooms are most associated with Japanese cuisine, but have now gained momentum in other types of cuisines as well. Enoki are unique in their taste and texture when compared to other mushrooms, as they are quite mild and don't overpower other flavors. What seems to be special about enoki, in my opinion, is how versatile they can be due to their ability to take on the taste of whatever dish they are being cooked in. These dainty, long-stemmed mushrooms provide a nice crunch when raw, and remain firm when cooked.

You can find them at Asian stores, although I have noticed they are becoming more popular in local grocery stores as well, but they are a great choice for the grower, because they are easy and fun to grow. These are often used in soups and noodle dishes, such as ramen bowls.

Description: Caps are generally on the smaller side from 0.5-2 inches, with long delicate stems around 2-5 inches tall. The caps look like small bulbs initially, but upon further development they will flatten out and even turn slightly upwards with age, but they are generally harvested before this happens. When grown at home, they are white in color, but occasionally bring on an off-white tinge. However, it should be noted that cultivated enoki look quite different to enoki grown in the wild where they take on a more golden-brown appearance.

Distribution and habitat: Enoki can be found in most temperate regions throughout the world, but are particularly common in Japan, China, and Korea. They grow on the stumps of hardwood trees.

Guidelines for growth: These mushrooms thrive in cold environments, and in the wild, they fruit during the winter season. They are even able to survive freezing temperatures, and will resume growth once thawed. Incubation periods are around 2 weeks long, at 72-77 °F. Spawning substrates are typically grain spawns, while the fruiting substrate is hardwood sawdust, generally supplemented. Fruiting temperatures can be quite low between 40-60 °F. They have even been known to fruit in refrigerators, as long as you give them fresh air throughout the day. Enoki will begin to fruit within 2-4 weeks of inoculation into the bulk substrate. These can be grown in polypropylene bags, or even cylindrical bottles. Humidity should be around 90%.

Enoki mushrooms growing in the wild

Enoki when grown indoors

MOREL (Morchella)

We've already covered a few unique mushrooms like Enoki and Lion's Mane, however, Morels are the pinnacle of mysteriousness in the mushroom world. These are tough to find in the wild, exhibiting evasive tendencies in the sense that they blend in to their surroundings extremely well, and only appear for a small number of days when and where they do pop up. Even the most experienced foragers have trouble finding Morels, as there isn't really a rhyme or reason as to why they show up where they do in terms of their seemingly random variety of habitats. These mushrooms exhibit an earthy, nutty flavor, and a meat-like texture. As a word of caution, these do tend to be quite difficult to grow at home, and people are often unsuccessful with many of the grow kits that are sold online.

Description: Shaped like cones with a ribbed texture resembling that of a honeycomb, Morels grow to be 1-3 inches wide, and 2-5 inches tall. These have a thick and hollow white stem that is coarse in texture.

Distribution and habitat: Morels grow throughout most temperate regions in the world. These can be found in an irregular variety of places in those regions, however. They have been known to thrive in areas that are recovering from fires, old apple orchards, and at the bases of both dead or decaying and live trees. You can also find Morels on south-facing hills where the conditions are moist and warm.

Guidelines for growth: Morels typically fruit in the springtime, when growing outdoors. Because these are nearly impossible to grow indoors, unless you have a high tech lab and a lot of experience, attempting to grow them outdoors by replicating their natural environment is your best bet.

Morel mushroom growing in the wild. A particularly hard variety to cultivate indoors

4

LET'S GET GROWING

GROWING MUSHROOMS AT HOME

*I*t should encourage you knowing that people have been growing mushrooms on a small scale for quite some time now, both indoors and outdoors. Many people have done it before you, which means there's no reason you shouldn't be able to also! By now you know that mushrooms are of various kinds, and several different forms of mushrooms grow in varying environments.

I have good news for those of you who live in small houses or apartments and feel that space is a must for this great hobby; it's not. Small places can provide perfect areas for mushroom growth. You can use spaces like a spare room, a basement, or even create a patch for your mushrooms in your vegetable garden. Finding space for growing mushrooms should not be what stops you.

Becoming a successful mushroom cultivator takes time, practice, and the ability to learn from your mistakes, but I promise you it is rewarding. In this chapter we'll go over the many different methods you can use to grow at home. We'll cover the different types of spawn and substrate and how to choose them, and we'll also discover the differences between pasteurization and sterilization, and lastly how to create ideal fruiting conditions.

GROWING KITS

As I previously discussed in Chapter 3, the easiest way you can grow mushrooms, especially when starting out, is by using growing kits. These are perfect for the novice grower as you are almost guaranteed to successfully grow mushrooms, as the brunt of the work is already done for you. These kits don't require any special skills or any certain equipment, and I highly recommend starting with one of these if you've never grown before. They are a great starting point to familiarize yourself with the process without having to actually do much yourself.

So how do we use grow kits? As a disclaimer, most kits will come with instructions for you to follow, and these should be used if provided. However, in general, the following instructions are a good rule of thumb to go by if your kit does not provide specific instructions.

After receiving the grow kit in the mail and unpacking it, you will see the fruiting block has been completely colonized with the mycelium. Firstly, you'll need to make a cut around 4 inches in length into the block with a knife, usually in the shape of an 'X.' This is to allow fresh air exchange, as well as giving the mushrooms somewhere to fruit, as they will grow toward their oxygen supply. Then, using the knife, scrape away the top layer of old mycelium to allow fresh mycelium to start growing.

The block will then need hydrating, to do this place the fruiting block with the cut side facing down into a bowl of water, this will in effect energize the mushrooms to start growing. Most kits will say to leave the block hydrating overnight, but again follow the kits specific instructions.

After leaving the fruiting block in a bowl of water overnight to hydrate, it is now ready to start fruiting. Take the block out of the water and choose the place where you want to see your mushrooms grow. Ideally, the indoor temperature should be somewhere around 65-70 °F, but bear in mind that the fungal growth will decline or completely diminish if the temperature is persistently below 60 degrees.

There are two other important factors to consider when using grow kits. Firstly, mushrooms need a lot of moisture when they are in the fruiting stage. Much like humans need food and water to survive, mushrooms need a substrate (food) and moisture (water). Failure to properly hydrate the substrate will cause your mushrooms to stop growing or greatly reduce the yield of mushrooms. Most grow kits will usually come with a spray to use, but a couple of sprays per day on your fruiting block should be enough to keep it sufficiently hydrated.

As well as adequate moisture, the other important factor to consider when using a grow kit is the amount of sunlight necessary, or should I say lack of sunlight. Grow kits will thrive best in areas of indirect sunlight. The results from using a grow kit can be very rewarding and surprisingly fast, which are great for getting started and giving you a little kick of motivation to grow on your own. After only a few days you should start to see little pinheads (the tiny stalks or as I call them the baby mushrooms). With each day you'll see your mushrooms growing at an impressive rate. After around 1-2 weeks, depending on the variety, your mushrooms will be ready to harvest. Simply use a knife to cut them at the base, or twist them off with your hands and there you have it–your gourmet mushrooms are ready for use.

However, the mycelium isn't finished there. With each fruiting block you can expect to get between 3-4 flushes until the mycelium has completely used up all the available energy from its substrate.

Mushroom kits are a great way for the novice grower to get started and can be a great boost in confidence to see your first successful harvest. If you're new to the whole idea of mushroom cultivation and are unsure where to start, start here. However, one word of caution I would like to mention is that of Morel grow kits. The morel mushroom is notoriously hard to grow even for experienced cultivators due to its sensitivity to temperature and moisture changes. Morel grow kits therefore have a bit of a reputation of being very hit and miss. I have used them myself on several occasions and have only successfully grown them once from a grow kit.

USING PREMADE SPAWN TO GROW MUSHROOMS

Earlier we defined spawn as the living fungal culture known as mycelium, grown onto a substrate. Any substance that has been inoculated with mushroom mycelium is known as mushroom spawn, however there are common substrates in the mushroom world that our favorite gourmet mushrooms grow best on. The substrate of choice will first need to be inoculated with the mushroom spores. Then, under the right incubation conditions the myelical network will start to take hold and slowly colonize the spawning substrate completely. Once the substrate has been fully colonized, it is then ready to be transferred to a fruiting substrate which will give rise to mushrooms.

For those wanting to challenge themselves a little more than using a grow kit but not quite to the full extent of making your own spawn, buying premade spawn is a great option. This will allow you to grow mushrooms and be more hands on without investing a ton of time or equipment in the beginning stages. I know several successful small scale and even large scale mushroom cultivators who simply buy premade spawn from a reputable supplier to save time and money by not having to make their own spawn. Another great benefit of this is the reliability that you are buying a healthy, fully colonized amount of spawning substrate which is ready to be inoculated into a fruiting substrate. They are also less susceptible to contamination as they have already taken hold of the spawning substrate. Of course, having said that, you do still have to practice cleanliness at all times when dealing with spawn.

Let's now discuss the 3 main types of spawn that you may come across when purchasing premade spawn.

TYPES OF SPAWN

Grain Spawn

Grains are the most commonly used substrate for making spawn. The grain is first sterilized to eliminate any microorganisms, then inoculated with the chosen variety of mycelium using spores either in liquid form in a syringe or from a culture grown on agar. The most commonly used grains are rye and millet, however there are also wheat grain spawns, and I have even heard of people using unpopped popcorn kernels as a type of grain spawn.

A great advantage of using a grain over sawdust for spawn is the nutritional value that it provides. Grains are much more nutritious than sawdust for all mushroom species. The mycelium feeds well on the high starch content that grains provide which makes it easier to colonize the whole substrate. A main disadvantage I always like to point out for prospective outdoor mushroom growers, however, is that because grains are an ideal food source for hungry rodents and birds, there is a chance they might decide to dig into your mushroom beds and eat the grains. This obviously isn't always the case, and you likely know your area best and whether or not this might occur there, but sometimes outdoor growers like to stick to sawdust spawn where possible.

If making your own spawn sounds like something you'd like to try, we'll go through a few step by step methods for doing so in Chapter 5!

Sawdust Spawn

As the name suggests, this spawn is made of sawdust that has been sterilized and then fully colonized with mycelium. Sawdust is a mixture of hardwood particles that are very fine, usually around a few millimetres in size. The small size of the sawdust particles gives it one of its best advantages over other spawn. Because of how small the particles are, they are able to make their way into every little crevice of the fruiting substrate. This allows the mycelial network to spread very quickly and colonize the entire mass of the substrate without allowing time for other competing microorganisms to compete.

The major disadvantage of having 100% sawdust as a spawn is that sawdust alone lacks many of the nutrients that other substrates have. This will lead to the mycelium running out of 'food' and can in turn lead to a reduction in yield as the mycelium quickly runs out of viable nutrition to keep it going. Luckily, the mushroom spawn producers have our backs and know how to get around this. There are supplements that can help. Just like supplements can help us humans improve performance, the same goes for sawdust spawn. Any type of bran (wheat bran, oat bran, or rice bran, most commonly) can greatly improve the quality and nutrition of the substrate by providing it with a higher nitrogen content which the mycelial networks thrive on.

Plug or Dowel Spawn

Plug spawn is the name given to a collection of very small wooden dowels that have been inoculated and colonized with mycelium. Often sawdust spawn is actually used to inoculate the wooden dowels. Purchasing plug spawn is a great option for those of you wanting to grow outdoors as they are perfect for inoculating logs, and the method is very simple which I will explain in Chapter 6.

Other Types of Spawn You May See

These are not very common, but you might come across them at some point in your mushroom journey.

Woodchip Spawn: This is made from wood chips of various hardwoods (has the same drawbacks as sawdust in relation to nutritional value)

Straw Spawn: This is pasteurized straw which has been inoculated and colonized with mycelium. However, straw tends to be used more often as a fruiting substrate.

Liquid Spawn/Spores: This is water that has been enriched with mycelium. Liquid spores are more commonly used to make your own spawn, which is explained in Chapter 5. They are generally not used to inoculate a fruiting substrate as they are not as effective in this manner.

Best Type of Mushroom Spawn?

There is not one type of spawn that comes out on top, and this is simply because the best type of spawn for any growing situation will depend on a number of key variables. As a general rule, try and match your spawn to your substrate. For example if you are wanting to grow mushrooms on wood chips, logs, or cardboard, then using a sawdust spawn would be best as they are both wood-based. Because the mycelium has already familiarized itself with the woody spawning substrate, colonization time of the fruiting substrate should decrease. Grain spawns tend to be most compatible with pasteurized straw or enriched sawdust (supplemented with a type of bran). And as we have just discussed, plug spawn is best for inoculating logs. The type of spawn you choose will also depend on the type of mushrooms you're growing. Each mushroom might grow better or worse on certain types of spawning and fruiting substrates. I'll break this down a bit more later on in this chapter.

Important points to note when buying spawn:

- Make sure to choose a reputable supplier, one that has a lot of good reviews. This will show that the quality of the mycelium is good thus increasing your chances of success. You would be surprised, but quality does vary between suppliers, so don't be put off if your first grow is unsuccessful. Keep looking, because it may just be that you need to source a new supplier for better quality spawn.
- When your spawn arrives, be ready to use it. Just because the spawn you have bought has fully colonized the substrate, this doesn't mean it can't go bad. Most spawn should have a 'use by' date which is usually within 6 weeks.
- If you can't use it straight away, then refrigerate it to reduce the chance of competing contaminants such as mold and bacteria spoiling your spawn.
- If you notice your spawn starts to turn any color other than white, then there is a high chance that it has been left too long and it has been contaminated. At that point, throw it away and order a new one.

I hope it was helpful discussing the different options regarding premade spawn. However, a mushroom is not going to grow without a fruiting substrate. This is sometimes referred to as a bulk substrate, and it is what you introduce your spawn to, so it can fully colonize it and eventually fruit from it. Below we will take a look at the different types of fruiting substrates you can use.

SUBSTRATES

What is a Mushroom substrate?

A mushroom substrate can be thought of as similar to that of what soil is to plants. Although the comparison is a logical one, the way in which mushrooms use a substrate compared to how plants use the soil is different and this needs to be understood when cultivating to achieve the best results. A substrate is any substance or material where the mushroom mycelium can establish and expand its network through decomposing the organic matter it is surrounded by. The primary purpose of this substrate is to provide the mycelium with a home where it finds key nutrients which aid it in its expansion and growth. The mushroom mycelium will work its way through the entirety of the substrate and eventually after absorbing all the nutrients, will have enough energy to fruit.

. . .

Choosing a Substrate

To grow mushrooms successfully, you need to choose the optimal substrate to grow your mushrooms on. We previously covered what each mushrooms favorite substrate, but here is a quick recap:

- Maitake: Hardwood sawdust
- Shiitake: Hardwood sawdust
- Lion's Mane: Hardwood sawdust supplemented with wheat bran
- King Oyster: Straw, sawdust, or master's mix
- Portobello/Button Mushroom: Manure or compost
- Enoki: Sawdust or master's mix
- Wine cap: Wood chips and straw in outdoor beds

Yes, I know it does look as though sawdust is the top substrate to use, but remember this is just a general guide. What makes growing mushrooms fun, is that you can mix and match and find out for yourself what works well and what doesn't, and choose what you prefer. So let's talk about the different substrates that are commonly used for growing mushrooms; remember, this is in regards to the fruiting or bulk substrate that you will be inoculating your spawn into, which will then give rise to your fruiting bodies.

· · ·

Commonly Used Mushroom Substrates

Mushrooms can grow on a wide range of substrates. There are a few substrates which are commonly used. Let's discuss each of them individually.

Straw

Straw is one of the most commonly used and readily available substrates that can be used. Many people don't actually know what straw is (I didn't before growing mushrooms), because it's not really something the average person needs to know. Straw is the agricultural byproduct of farming cereal grains such as wheat or barley, and it consists of the dry stalks of these plants after the grain and chaff have been removed. It's basically what's leftover after we have taken everything we need out of it. Because we take all the nutrition out of it, straw ends up not being the best option for many mushroom species. Nevertheless, straw can be a great choice for some species, most notably the Oyster family. Other species which do take well to straw include the Wine Cap and Lion's Mane. The beauty of straw is that it's easy to get your hands on and relatively inexpensive. You can pick up a bail of straw from a local farm (if you live near one this should be no problem), garden center, or even order it online.

. . .

Hardwood Sawdust and Pellets

Hardwood, as the name would suggest, is wood made from a variety of trees that are hard in nature. Trees such as beeches, oaks, and maples all fall under the hardwood variety. For your interest, and not growing purposes, types of softwood trees include pines, spruces and firs. Softwoods are not a good option for growing mushrooms as they have natural anti-fungal chemicals preventing substantial mycelium networks from forming. In the wild, many kinds of mushrooms use hardwood as a base for their growth (next time you're out and about have a look and take notice of which trees you find mushrooms growing on!). Common species that grow on hardwood include Shiitake, Maitake, Lion's Mane, Turkey Tail, Enoki, and Reishi. As previously discussed in the section regarding plug spawn, you can inoculate whole logs, however for growing indoors we use the finely ground hardwood mixture of sawdust that usually come in pellet form.

Hardwood sawdust is similar to straw in the sense that it is a byproduct, only this time it's a byproduct of the lumbar industry which again makes it a fairly inexpensive option to use as a substrate. For a more optimal substrate mix, you can enhance your sawdust with supplements which will be covered later on.

Coco Coir, Vermiculite and Gypsum Mix

Coco coir is a substance that is made of finely ground coconut husks and shells and is definitely growing in popularity in the mushroom world. You can get hold of some at most garden centres or in pet stores. They don't sell coco coir in great quantities as when it is soaked in water it will increase in size, many times the original amount. Coco coir is a great choice for growing mushrooms as it is naturally resistant to bacteria and molds, and is also great at retaining moisture. Vermiculite is a mineral that is yellow/brown in color and is most commonly used for growing hydroponic plants or aerating soil in garden beds. Because it lacks significant nutrition, it is generally mixed with other substrates, like coco coir, and sometimes brown rice flour. The purpose of using vermiculite as part of a mix in a substrate is due to its impressive ability to retain water. Vermiculite, like coco coir, can be easily found at most garden stores and pet stores. Coco coir and vermiculite when mixed together provide an adequate growing substrate, and you can create this mixture with a ratio of 1:1. The last ingredient for this mix is the gypsum, which is a sulfate mineral composed of calcium sulfate dihydrate. This is a great supplement for the substrate as it helps provide added calcium and sulfate which helps the mycelium grow. This should account for around 5-10% of the total substrate mix.

Coffee Grounds

Coffee grounds is something which I'm seeing more people grow with in recent years. You can get success using it as your sole substrate, however, in my opinion it is best used as a supplement to other substrates such as your hardwood sawdust. Coffee grounds are packed full of nitrogen making them a great energy source for the mycelium. The caveat is that coffee grounds are much more prone to contamination. For this reason, using them as your sole substrate is not the best option. Before using coffee grounds as a supplement to your substrate it will need be sterilized.

Manure and Compost

To many people, manure and compost might appear to be the best medium for growing mushrooms because they associate these with plant growth. I know before I got into growing I certainly thought this also. However, because mushrooms are not plants, majority of gourmet mushrooms that you might want to grow are not compatible with organic animal waste material. The common button mushroom is the exception to this, and it does very well growing on manure, compost, or a mixture of both. You have quite a few choices when it comes to manure selection; you can go for horse, cow, or even chicken manure. On a commercial scale the manure substrate goes through a complex process that allows the good microorganisms to come through while also killing off the bad and unwanted contaminants. This process also removes the ammonia that builds up through the composting phase. This is done to produce maximum yield. However, obviously most of you reading this book want to know low-tech methods that can be easily applied and are practical. Therefore, when using manure I will pasteurise it using boiling water, which I will explain later on in this chapter. Once it has been pasteurized, I mix the manure with vermiculite, gypsum and water (2 parts manure, 1 part vermiculite, 1 part water). Make sure that you mix well so all parts are combined thoroughly and evenly. Compost is generally already sterilized when bought in bags from garden centers, which makes it an easy option as well.

Cardboard

Cardboard is another substrate that is easily applicable. As a wood-based product, it is fairly nutritious—similar to the nutrition levels of the hardwood substrates. What's even better is that it is often easy to get for free. You can pick cardboard up from local restaurants and supermarkets that tend to have a lot of cardboard waste from shipments of stock they receive. An estimated 40% of the waste we throw away is suitable for growing mushrooms on, but it needs to be plain cardboard without any dyes or plastic on it. Cardboard also has the quality of moisture retention when soaked, and it allows for good air exchange. The more aggressive types of mushrooms grow easily on cardboard, such as oysters. By now you have probably realized that oyster mushrooms are an adaptable bunch and can take to most substrates fairly well.

Master's Mix

The master's mix is simply a 50/50 mix of soy hulls and hardwood sawdust, hydrated with water. Soy hulls are the outside layer of skin of the soybean, and are a byproduct of soybean farming. They provide great nutrition for mushrooms when mixed with sawdust. For a 5lb fruiting block, you'll want 1lb of hardwood sawdust and 1lb of the soy hulls, and to that you'll add 6 cups of water. Once you've mixed thoroughly and packed your substrate into your fruiting bags, you can then sterilize in a pressure cooker for 2.5 hours at 15psi and you're good to go! Master's mix works exceptionally well with oyster mushrooms, but can also be used for enoki and lion's mane. Feel free to experiment with other species and see how they do!

STERILIZATION VS. PASTEURIZATION

Now that we've gone over the many different possibilities for substrates, let's discuss two phrases in the mushroom world that you will hear a lot about pertaining to substrates–sterilization and pasteurization. These methods can be rather confusing if you're new to growing, and the two words are often thrown around interchangeably which is not always correct. Both of these methods essentially reduce the number of mold, bacteria and other potential contaminants to help make sure that the mushroom you are trying to grow can grow without competition and will therefore have a better chance at establishing its mycelial networks.

Pasteurization is a method that reduces the amount of existing microscopic competitors in a substrate. This is usually done by heating the substrate to temperatures of roughly 165°F or 175°C for a sustained period of time.

Sterilization, on the other hand, completely eliminates all microscopic competitors that might be present in a substrate, and is performed by heating the substrate to temperatures of roughly 250°F/121°C or higher, with a pressure cooker or autoclave at 15psi, also for a sustained period of time.

When growing mushrooms, certain substrates have to be sterile whereas others can just be pasteurized. The main factor to consider when deciding which method to use is to establish how nutrient-rich the substrate is. High-nutrient substrates (like grains, compost, manure, or supplemented sawdust) need to be sterilized because they are a likely food source for many different forms of bacteria and other microbial life, which equates to more competition for your mycelium to tackle. High-nutrient substrates attract many different types of mold and fungi, and an example of this is that you've probably seen food in your kitchen start growing mold after just a week or two. Low-nutrient substrates (like unsupplemented sawdust, straw, cardboard), however, can get away with only being pasteurized because they are not an appealing food source for competitors.

A helpful way I think about it, is anything which could be considered a food source for a wild animal should be sterilized to ensure the best chance for your mushroom mycelium to grow. When using substrates which have been enriched using supplements, they will need sterilizing and not just pasteurizing. This is because supplements are nitrogen rich and are more likely to be home to the microscopic organisms which will lead to contamination.

There are a few different methods for sterilization and pasteurization which I will go over now.

STERILIZING WITH A PRESSURE COOKER/AUTOCLAVE:

When sterilizing using a pressure cooker or autoclave, you are essentially just placing your fruiting blocks or jars of spawning substrate (which will be in polypropylene bags or glass jars that are heat resistant) into the pressure cooker and letting them sit in the pressure cooker for a certain amount of time, depending on what you're sterilizing, and at 15psi. This will kill off any bacteria, mold, or other fungi that may have been present. For example, if you plan on growing using supplemented sawdust, you would mix the sawdust, the supplement, and the water (according to the required proportions), then pack the mix into the polypropylene bags (spawn is always added after sterilization). Once the substrate is packed down, you will fold down the lip of the bag to seal it, then place it into the pressure cooker to sterilize the bag. I'll explain this in more detail in one of the methods later in this chapter so you know how to do it properly. Grains that are used for making spawn also need to be sterilized in a pressure cooker. You can place the grains in mason jars, then place them into the pressure cooker, and again, let them sterilize for the necessary time at 15psi.

An important note with pressure cookers is that you want to make sure you fill it with enough water. If there isn't enough water in it, the temperature and pressure can become dangerously high inside, and will have the potential to explode (very worst case), or burn and melt whatever is inside. To avoid any serious problems, just make sure you've placed enough water in the bottom of the pot, which you will get used to over time. Be aware of the steam vent, and if you notice that steam stops coming out, turn the heat off and let it cool.

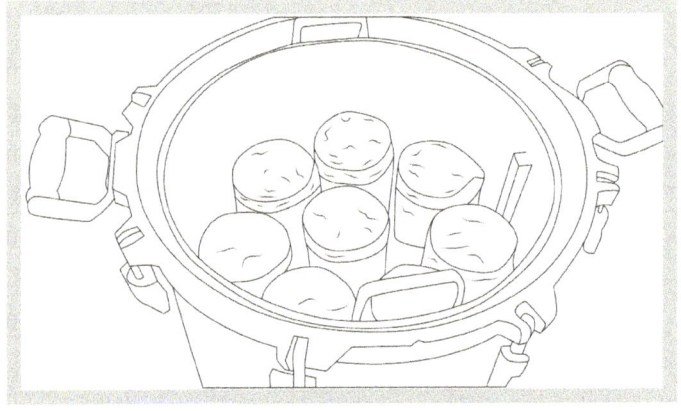

Pressure cooker with jars of grain spawn placed inside

Of course, not everyone has access to a pressure cooker or autoclave, so there are ways to get around this step when home-growing. For fruiting substrates, like straw or sawdust, you can pasteurize instead. However, if you don't have a pressure cooker, I wouldn't recommend using supplements, as they are too high in nutrients to get away with just pasteurization. If you plan on pasteurizing using the methods below, you will need to use pure sawdust, or pure straw. For grains to be used as a spawning substrate, you can use a low-tech method called PF Tek to sterilize, which I will take you through, step by step, in the next chapter. But first, let's go over two different pasteurization methods.

PASTEURIZING

You can pasteurize substrates using cold or hot water. Some people find the hot water method preferable as it takes less time. However, both provide the same end result so it doesn't necessarily matter which one you choose–it's up to you.

Pasteurizing Using Hot Water

1. The straw needs cutting up into small 1-2 inch pieces. You can do this with a large food processor blender, if you're growing indoors and only need a small amount, or if you're using large amounts, you can place the straw in a big drum or barrel outside and shred it with a weed whacker. This is an important step as it will allow the mycelium from the spawn to more easily colonize the smaller pieces.
2. Rinse the cut up pieces of straw with cold water, to remove any dirt.
3. Pasteurising occurs at temperatures between

160-180 °F (71-82 °C). Bring a pot of water to the boil and then come off the heat until you are at a temperature of between 160-180 °F.

4. Put the straw into a nylon mesh bag and submerge under the water. All the straw needs to be under the water, so place something heavy on top like a plate or bowl. You can use a thermometer to make sure that the temperature stays between the recommended range.

5. Leave for between 1-2 hours, then remove the bag from the pot and place in a strainer to let the straw drain.

6. Once drained, lay the straw out to dry. You don't want it to be bone dry because the spawn will need it to be moist. A good way of testing this is with the squeeze test. If you squeeze it and there's still water coming out, you need to let it dry longer, but it still needs to be on the moist side.

7. Now you're ready to inoculate with your spawn!

PASTEURIZATION USING COLD WATER AND LIME

The heat of the water has the effect of reducing the number of potential contaminants when using the hot water pasteurization method, so if we only have cold water this will have no effect on the number of contaminants. Therefore, when pasteurizing with cold water, we have to use hydrated lime which will provide the same effect as hot water. Hydrated lime is the chemical compound known as Calcium Hydroxide and it is used for a variety of things including in the production of plasters, paints and cements. It's useful for pasteurization as it causes the pH of water to increase considerably (up to around 11-12 pH) which causes many competing microorganisms to die off. However, you need to choose the correct hydrated lime to do the job. There is a type of hydrated lime that you can pick up from garden centres fairly easily which is usually used to treat garden soils, but unfortunately, this type won't work because it is too weak and won't raise the pH of the water high enough. Therefore, your best bet is to purchase it online. You need to look for hydrated lime high in Calcium Hydroxide (upwards of 90%) and not Calcium Carbonate. You also need to make sure you purchase hydrated lime which is low in magnesium, as too high of a magnesium concentration can greatly reduce the myceliums ability to grow. You should also obtain litmus paper, which you can buy online as well. This is a special type of paper which changes color according to pH levels when dipped into liquid.

I would like to stress an important point about using hydrated lime here. It is a strong chemical that can cause rashes and skin burns and getting any in your eyes can cause serious problems. When handling this chemical, please remember to use gloves, safety glasses, and a mask to cover your mouth and nose to prevent any unwanted side effects.

Alright, now let's go over the method:

1. Cut up the straw cut up into small 1-2 inch pieces and wash it to remove any obvious contaminants (same step as before).
2. Fill up a large plastic tub/bucket full of cold water and add your hydrated lime to the water. For every 1 litre of water add 3-4 grams of hydrated lime and mix well.
3. Test the pH of your water–you are aiming to get it between 11-12 pH.
4. Once you are happy with the pH, add your straw to the lime and water mix.
5. Once again, straw has a tendency to float and we need it to be fully submerged in the water, so put a heavy object on top of the straw such as a bin with logs in it to keep it submerged.
6. Now, you can let the hydrated lime do its thing. Leave it to pasteurize for between 12-24 hours.
7. After this time, remove the straw and let it drain. Again we want it fairly dry but not too dry. You can do the squeeze test for this as well to assess the straw moisture levels.

8. Once you have let it dry appropriately you can then inoculate it with your mushroom spawn and you are ready to grow.

Both of the above methods for pasteurizing straw work very well, and of course you can use exactly the same method and substitute in a different substrate such as unsupplemented sawdust, as stated earlier.

PASTEURIZING WITH A MICROWAVE, BOILING WATER, OR AN OVEN

Now let's cover how you can pasteurize manure or compost. We've got three options; boiling water, the oven, or the microwave. They are all extremely simple steps and although some growers out there might look at this as an unnecessary step, you can never be too careful in preventing contamination.

For obvious reasons I have only ever tried the microwave method with compost, as I don't know about you, but I don't fancy manure in my microwave (but feel free if you're brave enough)! All you need to do is load up a bowl full of compost and place it in the microwave for around 10 minutes on high. The compost will come out piping hot and your compost will now be pasteurized. The obvious downside to this method is it takes quite a few turns in the microwave to get enough compost to use as a substrate.

Similar to my microwave, I've only tried compost in my oven. For this method, you'll need an aluminum baking tray. Fill it with your compost, or manure, and cover it with tin foil. Next, place it in the oven for an hour, at 175 °F. Start the timer after the oven has fully heated to 175 degrees.

To pasteurize compost or manure using boiling water, the method is equally as simple. This can be done outside using one of our trusty big plastic containers. Add your compost or manure to the container and slowly add the boiling water and mix thoroughly. Keep filling up with water until the substrate is of 'gloopy' consistency, not too stiff and not too runny. Then place a cover over the container and let it sit for around 10-15 minutes. After this period of time, the boiling water and the steam (created from the cover) will have done the trick and your substrate will be pasteurized.

Keep in mind that the only way to truly sterilize your substrates are by using a pressure cooker or an autoclave, as these are the only way to get high enough pressures to kill off all contaminants.

Adding supplements to substrates

I have already briefly discussed that supplements can be added to your substrate in order to provide beneficial nutrients to your mushrooms. The primary purpose of using supplements is to enhance the yield. When using supplements, the mycelium can grow both quicker and larger. This results in a shorter harvesting time and a greater overall size of mushroom fruiting bodies. However, there is a caveat to adding supplements and that is; the more you add, the greater the risk of contamination. There is a wide range of nitrogen rich elements that can be used to boost the nutritional efficacy of the base substrate. The most commonly used supplements include wheat bran, oat bran, coffee grounds, maize powder, and rice bran. When adding a supplement to a substrate, it's best to mix in 10% supplement and 90% substrate (dry weight), however if you are concerned with contamination either steer clear of supplements altogether or go for a 5% supplement to 95% substrate mix. I use rice bran when supplementing which has around 12-15% protein content and 2% nitrogen. All supplements have a slightly different protein and nitrogen content. Please see below for the breakdown of the most commonly used supplements. You should err on the side of caution with supplements that have a higher protein and nitrogen content, and add less and not more, until you have established a good substrate to supplement ratio. You do not want to risk over-supplementation which may lead to contamination. If you decide to add a supplement to your substrate then it should go through a longer sterilization process.

· · ·

List of Supplements and Their Protein and Nitrogen Concentrations:

Rice Bran: 12-15% Protein. 2% Nitrogen.

Wheat Bran: 10% Protein. 1.5% Nitrogen.

Oat Bran: 17% Protein. 2.5% Nitrogen

Coco Coir: 15% protein. 2.5% Nitrogen.

Coffee Grounds: 8-12% Protein. 2% Nitrogen

What to do with your finished substrate:

Many growers seem to feel this is a problematic step, and feel wasteful having to throw it away. However, the last thing you should be doing is throwing it in the garbage. Spent substrate can be recycled into a composting patch or if you have a garden straight into the soil. If you have been growing aggressive species such as Oysters, and if you're lucky, you may find in 6 months to a year that you get a fresh batch of mush-rooms coming through, and once they are established they will keep growing back year after year!

TIME TO GROW MUSHROOMS!

Now that we've covered the basics, we can get on and learn some great, easy to apply methods for growing a variety of mushrooms on different substrates!

GROWING OYSTER MUSHROOMS ON STRAW

Oyster mushrooms are arguably the most beginner friendly mushroom to grow, being an extremely hardy and versatile species. King Oysters and Blue Oysters are my personal favorite and are a great option if you're just starting out. The first two things you need to do is to purchase your ready made spawn from a reputable supplier and to source your straw which has been previously discussed.

Growing oyster mushrooms on straw is a rewarding process and one that can be easily replicated at home, no matter how big or small your place is. Recently moving into an apartment I have grown using low tech methods with limited space, and have still produced some exciting results.

Below is a list of exactly what you will need:

- Straw, 2kg (dry weight)
- Grow bags (These can be easily sourced online. They are sturdy polypropylene bags which have an air vent at the top which allows for

good airflow but prevents contaminants from
entering)
- Oyster mushroom spawn, 250 grams
- Spray bottle for misting
- Large pot (for the pasteurization)
- Mesh bag

Method:

1. Always start your mushroom growing process
   by cleaning your workspace as outlined in
   Chapter 2, and washing your hands (and any
   equipment that you will be using) thoroughly.
2. Before we think about pasteurizing, we first
   need to establish how much straw we need.
   Your ratio of spawn to substrate should be 10%
   minimum (i.e. if you have 100 grams of grain
   spawn you should have a maximum of 1kg of
   dry straw). The less straw you have the more
   easily the mycelium will colonize. Weigh out
   your straw and then you are good to start the
   pasteurization process. *Note the
   measurements above are for using 250 grams
   of spawn, this can be varied depending upon
   how much you want to make, just make sure
   you have at least 10% spawn, ideally 15-20%.
3. Please follow the guide from the section about
   pasteurization to correctly pasteurize your

straw. You can use either hot or cold water pasteurization.

4. Once you have completed the pasteurization process and you are happy that your straw has the right moisture content, then it is time to inoculate it with the spawn. Before adding the spawn to the straw it is important to break up the spawn into small pieces that will mix well into the substrate. This gives the mycelium a better chance to colonize the straw more evenly.

5. The best way to achieve great results with inoculation is to thoroughly mix your spawn in with your pasteurized straw by hand (thoroughly washed hands, or using clean, new latex gloves) to get an even distribution of spawn throughout the straw. If doing this outside you can do this in a big (clean) barrel, or you can do this inside in a large bowl (you may have to do it in several batches).

6. Once the spawn and the substrate have been properly mixed, it is time to fill up your grow bags. You can simply do this by hand and you want to pack the straw down as much as you can. Packing it down as much as you can will prevent any air pockets from forming and thus, prevent any pinning from occurring on the inside of the bag. We want them pinning (or forming baby mushrooms) outside of the bag

when we introduce fruiting conditions later on. Once you have filled your bags up, push the last bit of air out the grow bag and tie the top tightly, or fold it down a few times. If your grow bag has an air patch filter, then that is sufficient for colonization. If not, you will need to poke a few small holes around the sides of your bag to allow your mycelium to breathe.

7. Now the hard part has been completed, you can sit back and relax while your oyster mushrooms start to colonize the straw. The colonization process will take between 1-2 weeks. Your bags should be kept in a room with minimal sunlight and at room temperature, or in a room that gets slightly warmer than the rest of your house if possible. You also should consider placing it somewhere with enough airflow. Keep in mind, if the temperature of the room is too hot (over 90 °F), the mycelium will likely die.

8. If you are hanging your bags, you can poke a few holes in the bottom and place a bucket underneath the bag to allow drainage of the substrate.

9. You should check your bags every couple of days to look for any signs of contamination, any green or bright blue colors or bad smells are signs that there is contamination. However, if you have done your part with keeping your

workspace clean and sterile, then this hopefully won't be an issue. You should see nice clear white mycelium slowly colonising your straw substrate.

10. After 1-2 weeks your mushrooms are ready to fruit when the entire bag is fully covered in white mycelium. That is your mushrooms telling you they're ready to pin! The best fruiting conditions can be inside or outside with an indirect light source. A good option is to hang your bags and if you haven't already done so, to cut holes in the side of them (Either poking holes or cutting an 'X' in the side of them). Around 8 holes is a good number to go for. You can also place your fruiting bags in a *shotgun fruiting chamber* (I will explain what this is, at the end of this chapter).

11. Within a few days of fresh air exposure, you should start to notice your mushrooms pinning. You can think of these as baby mushrooms. You will be amazed from this point how quickly your mushrooms will grow, sometimes doubling in size every 1-2 days. After about a week your mushrooms will be ready to harvest!

12. Try to harvest your mushrooms before they are about to drop their spores. You can identify this as mushrooms disperse their spores when their cap curls upwards. To harvest, simply cut

your mushrooms at the base of the stem and then let the bag be, and around a week later you should be able to harvest yet again. You might be able to get 3-4 harvests with one grow bag.

GROWING OYSTER MUSHROOMS ON COCO COIR, VERMICULITE AND GYPSUM.

Earlier we discussed how Coco Coir and vermiculite can be a great substrate to use for some mushrooms. If I were to use this as my substrate I would most likely grow Oysters on it however, I have also used this substrate to grow Lion's Mane.

Here is what you'll need for this growing method:

- 650 gram brick of coco coir
- 6 cups of vermiculite
- 1 cup of gypsum
- 18 cups of water
- Oyster mushroom spawn (At least 800 grams of spawn)
- Large 5 gallon drum bucket (Or an equivalent sized bucket)

Method:

1. Start by putting your block of coco coir, 6 cups of vermiculite, and gypsum into a large bucket.

2. Measure out 15 cups of water into a saucepan and bring to the boil.

3. Once your water has boiled, pour in the water to the bucket. Cover the top of the bucket with a lid if you have one for the bucket, or with some aluminium foil, and leave for 6-8 hours.

4. After you have left it for the stated time you will notice that once you take the lid off, your coco coir substrate mix will have expanded by about 10 times. Get in there with a pair of gloves and give the substrate a good mix around.

5. You want to make sure that there is not too much moisture, so do the squeeze test to determine moisture content. Get a handful and squeeze as hard as you can, you should see a couple of drops come out but there shouldn't be a heavy stream of water. If your substrate has too much moisture, you should allow it to dry for a while longer.

6. Once the substrate has the right moisture content you are now ready to inoculate. Break up your premade spawn into small even pieces in the packet, and thoroughly mix it into the substrate.

7. The mycelium now needs to colonize the substrate in the same conditions we talked

about before, for 1-2 weeks in a dark room with indirect sunlight and the temperature between 20-24 °C (71-75 °F).

8. Check your bucket regularly and when you see the top has turned into a white layer over the top then you are read for fruiting.

9. Poke several holes in the side of the bucket and hang outside again in indirect sunlight. Keep your mycelium hydrated by using a mister (or something similar) every day.

10. After 1-2 weeks or so your mushrooms should be ready for harvest.

GROWING SHIITAKE MUSHROOMS ON SAWDUST

Shiitake mushrooms are another great species to grow at home and can be extremely rewarding for both novice and expert alike. These mushrooms are a little bit more challenging but who doesn't like a challenge every once in a while! In your progress as a mushroom cultivator, this is a great addition to your skill set. The mycelium of shiitake mushrooms is not as rapid in growth as that of oyster mushrooms, so their incubation period is longer. However, the best part about growing shiitake mushrooms is that their yield can be greater than the oyster mushrooms. Shiitake mushrooms can easily produce 3 to 5 flushes on average from one substrate once it starts fruiting.

Here is what you will need for this grow:

- Shiitake spawn
- Sawdust (Amount will depend on grams of premade spawn. Remember at minimum, 10% spawn for your substrate)
- Supplement (Such as rice bran, *optional)
- Grow bags

Method:

1. Firstly, you need to source you Shiitake spawn,

your sawdust (or sawdust pellets) and bran (optional).

2. The sawdust now needs pasteurizing (if you decide to use a supplement such as a bran with your sawdust, this will need sterilizing–please see the section about pressure cookers for directions on how to do this, and also take a look at the method for sterilization which is included in the section for growing lion's mane on sawdust, coming up next).

3. Once the sawdust mix has been pasteurized it should be drained and then left to cool for a couple of hours. Perform the squeeze test to determine moisture content.

4. Now in a large bowl or big plastic container mix your mycelium spawn and sawdust well so the spawn is evenly distributed throughout.

5. You are now ready to fill your grow bags up. Tightly pack your sawdust and spawn mixture down into the bags.

6. Once they are full, press the air out and then tie the bag up tightly at the top. (Again if you have the grow bags with the air filter at the top then you don't need poke holes, but if there is no air ventilation pocket then you do need to poke a few holes around the top to allow your mushrooms to breathe).

7. Unlike Oyster mushrooms, Shiitake mushroom colonization will take anywhere between 6-12

weeks. Place your grow bags in a dark but well ventilated room.

8. After 6-12 weeks you will notice your substrate become fully colonized with white mycelium, but contrary to Oyster mushrooms this is not the time to fruit Shiitakes just yet. You need to allow another couple of weeks until they start to brown and you can see small pins forming under the plastic.

9. With adequate browning of around half of the substrate, it is now ready to fruit. A technique called 'shocking' can be used to wake up the mushrooms and lead to an improved flush. Give the bag a few hard slaps on all sides of the bag and then leave it overnight in your fridge for 12-36 hours. This shocks the mycelium into fruiting faster. If you do not have space in your fridge, then alternatively you can leave the fruiting block in your garage, or outside if it's cold enough.

10. After taking it out of the fridge it is now ready to fruit. You need to take the whole block out of the bag. Cut across the top of the bag and remove your ready to fruit block. *Top Tip: For some reason I found out that Shiitake fruiting blocks perform much better when turned upside down. I tried it once and have never looked back, try it out for yourself.

11. Keep your fruiting block in an area which is

humid and has lots of fresh air. *Top Tip: You can buy an air humidifier and turn it on for a couple hours per day, your Shiitakes will really appreciate this. You can also place it in a shotgun fruiting chamber.

12. Misting is required throughout the fruiting phase. Once or twice a day is plenty. You should see your fruiting block turn from a light brown to a dark brown. You need to keep the substrate moist. Shiitake mushrooms take in a lot of water and grow faster and healthier when adequately hydrated. After around one week your Shiitakes should be ready for harvest.

13. The best way to harvest your shiitake mushroom is to cut them from the bottom. Do not try to twist them since that might damage the mycelium and will impact future growth. A good time to tell when they are ready is when the caps are still rounded but look to be flattening. You can either cut them all off at the same time or just cut off the larger ones.

14. You can get up to 5 flushes of Shiitakes from one fruiting block, depending on the size of your block of course. However, the method to do this is rather different to other mushroom species. You need to let them have a resting period for 2-3 weeks. After this time soak them in a tub of water to rehydrate them and then

you are ready to repeat the cycle (hit, fridge, fruit!).

GROWING LION'S MANE USING SAWDUST

As I said earlier, Lion's Mane mushrooms are not only beautiful to look at but are also very tasty, and are said to have numerous health benefits. They are unique because of their meaty texture and crab-like taste, and because of that, they are a really fun one to grow at home! Lion's Mane has become quite popular in recent years as a culinary treat and many mushroom growers spend their time specifically growing this mushroom, either for themselves, or to sell. I prefer growing lion's mane mushrooms indoors on sawdust, but they can also be grown on logs outdoors, which I'll explain in Chapter 6.

There are two ways to grow Lion's Mane on sawdust, depending on whether or not you plan on supplementing your substrate, and whether or not you have a pressure cooker. If you do want to supplement your sawdust block with something like wheat bran, you'll need to sterilize it as the wheat bran would make it a high-nutrient substrate. However, if you just want to use pure sawdust, you can go a bit more low-tech and just pasteurize it using one of the methods from the pasteurization section earlier in this chapter. Once you have pasteurized your substrate, you can start from step 6 below.

If you do have a pressure cooker and want to supplement your sawdust, your first step is going to be making the fruiting blocks.

Here's what you'll need for that:

- Sawdust (5 cups)
- Wheat bran (1 cup)
- Water (6 cup)
- Polypropylene fruiting/growing bags

1. Combine all of the ingredients above into a large plastic container and mix very thoroughly to ensure an even distribution. Keep slowly adding water until you see that the mixture cannot absorb any more water. You want the mixture to be moist, but not soggy. You can perform the squeeze test again here to make sure you don't have too much water– remember, water should barely be dripping out when this is done.

2. Once you have achieved the correct moisture level, pack the mixture down into a fruiting bag into the shape of a rough block. Seal the bag by folding it down a couple times, ensuring that the filter patch is facing outwards.

3. Place the fruiting blocks into a pressure cooker,

with water about halfway up the sides of the bags that are nearest to the bottom of the cooker. You don't want the water to be so high that it leaks into the bags. Some pressure cookers will come with a metal plate or rack that you can place on the bottom so that the bags are not directly touching the bottom of the canner, but if yours does not, you can also use the lids of mason jars or something similar that can prevent the bags from directly touching the bottom. Place something heavy over the bags to keep them folded down – this can be an upside down plate, for example.

4. Now you're ready to seal the pressure cooker and place it on the stove/hob. Turn the heat up to medium/high and allow the pressure to reach 15psi, then you can turn the heat down to medium/low to low for the remainder of the process. The sterilization process should continue for 2.5 hours to ensure no unwanted substances are left in the substrate. The timer for the 2.5 hours should start only after the pressure cooker has reached 15psi.

5. After the sterilization process, let the block of sawdust cool completely before you start inoculation.

6. Before inoculation, clean your workspace and your hands thoroughly to limit the chance of contamination.

7. Get your mushroom spawn and add it to the sawdust block. Mix it well to ensure a thorough and even distribution of spawn throughout the block. For 5 lbs of substrate, you want 1 lb of spawn.

8. Your bag should then be placed in a dark and warm place to grow. The mycelium will be white initially but may become a light brown as it starts to spread, so don't be alarmed if this happens. Lion's Mane blocks should take around 2-3 weeks to colonize.

9. Once the bag is completely colonized with mycelium, create several holes around the bag roughly ¼-1 inch to an inch in size to induce fruiting. Don't forget to either use a shotgun fruiting chamber to maintain humidity levels, and fan for fresh air exchange, or hang indoors or outdoors in indirect sunlight and mist a few times daily. You should start to see pins on the mycelium within a week or so.

GROWING OYSTER MUSHROOMS ON CARDBOARD

We have already discussed growing oyster mushrooms on straw and on sawdust. Another great way of growing them is using cardboard. As I have previously mentioned, you can use old cardboard that you would usually recycle; shipment boxes, packages in the mail or any other cardboard that you otherwise don't need. Remember to avoid large amounts of dye or any plastic tapes.

Here is what you will need:

- Spray bottle
- A kettle or pot to boil water in
- Cardboard
- A bucket or a pot
- Oyster spawn

I like to grow pink oyster mushrooms on cardboard, however you can also grow blue oysters. Both are easy to grow, the only difference lies in their requirement of temperature. Blue oyster mushrooms require a cooler temperature which is somewhere around 10-20 °C. Pink oyster mushrooms require a tropical temperature which can be around room temperature 22-24 °C (71-75 °F).

. . .

Method:

1. You need to start by pasteurizing the cardboard. Cut your cardboard pieces up into roughly 3 inch by 3 inch pieces and place in your bucket. Bring the kettle or pot of water to the boil. Once boiled, pour the water over the cardboard until fully covered. Place a heavy object on top of the cardboard to submerge. Put the lid on the container and leave it for around 2 hours.

2. After this period of time your cardboard will be pasteurized. Drain the cardboard and let it sit for around 10 minutes. There's no need to perform the squeeze test using cardboard as a bit of excess moisture is fine when using cardboard, it will actually help the spawn to stick to it.

3. A layering technique is best used when cardboard is your substrate. Break up the mushroom spawn and sprinkle at the base of your bucket. Then add roughly a ½-1 inch thick layer of cardboard. Keep layering your bucket with some spawn and then cardboard until you have used up both and your tub is tightly packed.

4. The mycelium needs to be left to colonize the cardboard substrate for about 2 weeks. Cut some holes in the side of your bucket, which

will initially be for air ventilation and eventually the site your Oysters will come out of. Place a lid on the bucket and place in a dark room.

5. After 2 weeks you should see that your substrate is now white and ready to fruit. Place outside into fresh air and after a week or so you should have Oyster mushrooms coming through. Don't forget to maintain moisture levels by misting.

6. Harvest when you feel you have good enough growth and enjoy the tasty treat!

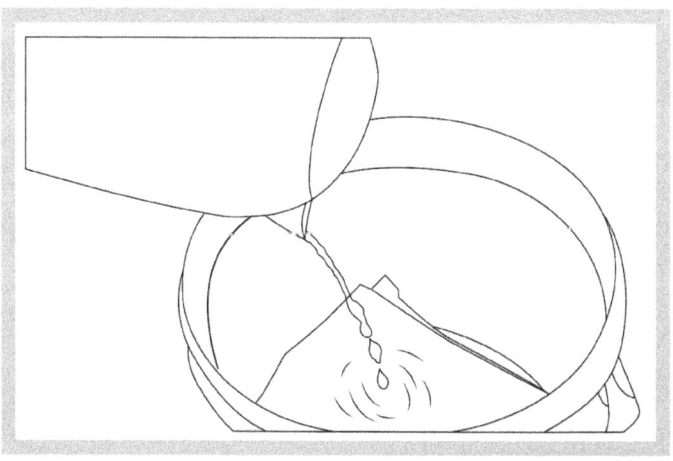

Pour boiling water over the cardboard into a bucket and leave to pasteurise for 1-2 hours. (Step 1)

GROWING ENOKI IN MASON JARS

This is one of my favorite methods of growing, and Enoki are one of my favorite types of mushrooms to eat. There's just something that is oddly satisfying about growing mushrooms out of bottles or jars. This method works well for Oysters and Maitake as well, and can be used for some others, but not for Shiitake. There are plastic bottles that can be bought for this method online, but I prefer to use quart-sized mason jars because they are a little easier to find in my experience. Enoki mushrooms grow best on hardwood sawdust, so that's what we'll be using for this method.

Again, there are two ways you can do this one, depending on whether or not you have a pressure cooker. If you don't have a pressure cooker, and you plan on using pure sawdust, you can pasteurize it using either one of the cold or hot water methods. Once pasteurized, fill the mason jars, not packed too tightly, up to the rim of the jar, and perform step 4, then continue from step 6 below.

If you do have a pressure cooker, you'll want to supplement your hardwood sawdust and sterilize it.

Here's what you'll need:

- Hardwood sawdust (5 cups)
- Wheat bran (1 cup)

- Water (6 cups)
- Enoki spawn (or other mushroom spawn of choice)
- Quart sized mason jars with lids
- Poly stuffing (pillow stuffing)

Method:

1. You'll first want to drill holes into the lids of each jar, roughly ¼ inch in diameter, then fill the hole with poly stuffing to act as a filter and allow the mycelium to breath.

2. Get a large container to mix together the hardwood sawdust, wheat bran, and water. Add the water slowly and mix thoroughly so the ingredients are fully and evenly distributed. You know the drill by now–you don't want the substrate to be too moist.

3. Once the substrate is mixed well and you've achieved the correct moisture levels, fill the mason jars to the bottom of the rim of the jar. They don't need to be packed too tightly, but do make sure there is enough substrate in them. You can tap the bottom of the jars on the table to help them compact down a little.

4. Use the end of a long wooden spoon, or anything similar, to tunnel a hole down the middle of the jar, all the way to the bottom. This will allow the spawn to work its way onto the substrate from the inside out.

5. Now you can place these into your pressure cooker. Be gentle handling the jars, as you don't want the hole in the middle to collapse. Make sure you've placed the metal separating plate/rack or more mason jar lids at the bottom

of the pressure cooker so that your jars are not directly touching the bottom of the cooker. Fill with water up to slightly below the neck of the jars closest to the bottom. Sterilize the jars at 15psi for at least 1.5 hours. Once sterilized, let the jars fully cool before inoculating.

6. In a still air box, fill the hole in the center with your mushroom spawn. The reason we do this is because with how full the jars are, it's not possible to really mix the spawn into the substrate practically. If you don't have a still air box, there are instructions on how to make one in Chapter 5.

7. Incubate at room temperature, away from direct sunlight, like in a closet or on a shelf in your pantry. Colonization should take roughly 3-4 weeks. This takes a bit longer than usual because the spawn is not mixed into the substrate.

8. Once fully colonized, it's time to remove the lid and scrape off the top layer of the mycelium to allow for even pinning, and place in fruiting conditions. You can definitely a use a shotgun fruiting chamber for this method as well. Enoki like cold environments, so try to find a place where you can keep them around 50-55 °F. You can place the lid back on loosely, or place a wet cloth over the top of the jar, to induce pinning. Once pinning starts, you can then remove the

lid completely and wait for the mushrooms to fully form!

Quart sized mason jar filled with sawdust—don't forget to only fill the jar with sawdust to the bottom of the rim.(Step 3)

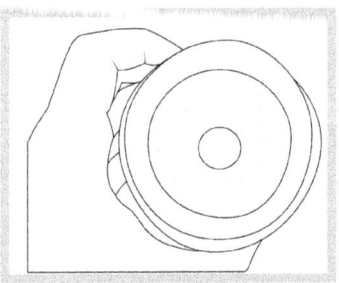

Hole made by tunnelling down with wooden spoon handle in center of sawdust (Step 4)

Oyster mushrooms also grow well out of bottles

GROWING BUTTON MUSHROOMS ON COMPOST (INDOORS)

Button mushrooms grow well on compost and this can easily be done indoors in large plastic totes/containers (monotub fruiting chambers). Some people choose to pasteurize the compost in an oven prior to inoculation, by placing it in a tin baking tray and baking it at the lowest temperature, or around 160-180 °F.

Here's what you'll need for this grow:

- Button mushroom spawn
- Compost (Can get from garden center)
- Gypsum (10% of substrate)
- Vermiculite (10% of substrate)
- A large plastic box container, rectangle shape.

Method:

1. First of all you need to obtain some compost, which can easily be sourced from your local garden center. Compost from a garden store is sterilized before being bagged, so you don't necessarily need to pasteurize it again unless you know it hasn't been sterilized, or it's a bag

that has been sitting out in the open for a while prior to using it.

2. Make sure your bucket has been thoroughly cleaned before adding the compost. Add your compost, with 10% vermiculite and 10% gypsum to the bucket so it is ⅔'s full and mix your dry ingredients well before adding any water.

3. Add a cup of water to your dry mix and stir in so it is all mixed well. Keep adding water to your mix until you are satisfied with the moisture content of your mix. Cue the squeeze test.

4. Once you're satisfied with your water content, add your mushroom spawn to your substrate and mix together. Remember you want at least a 10% ratio of spawn to substrate, but 15-20% is preferable where possible.

5. Leave your box in a room with minimal sunlight and at room temperature for a few weeks. You can check on them every couple of days and lightly mist them to keep them damp.

6. After a couple of weeks you should notice the webbing of the mycelium across the top of the compost. A great tip now is to 'case' the mycelium, by adding a 2-3 inch layer of damp compost on top of the mycelium.

7. If possible for fruiting, lower the temperature of the bed, by placing it in the garage or a

cooler room (around 15 °C or 60 °F). This is not essential but helps get a larger harvest.

8. After around another month or so you will start to see your first little white button mushroom caps poking their heads through. Your button mushrooms are ready to harvest when their caps look fully formed as you would find them at the supermarket. To harvest, simply twist the stems and they should come right out.

CREATING IDEAL FRUITING CONDITIONS

Depending on the type of mushroom you are growing, there are a few different options that you have for creating ideal fruiting conditions. Some people choose to fruit directly from the grow bags without any sort of fruiting chamber, and this can be done in rooms that are kept at a warm enough temperature with indirect sunlight.

Others prefer to use monotubs, shotgun fruiting chambers, or a martha indoor fruiting chamber.

Monotubs are the most commonly used type of fruiting chamber which are implemented by small-scale home growers. The setup is very simple, consisting of a large plastic container/storage box with a few holes drilled in the sides for ventilation. An inoculated substrate is placed directly into the tub for fruiting. These are most commonly used for mushrooms that grow upwardly like button mushrooms, as you have just read.

Shotgun fruiting chambers are similar to monotubs in that they are a large plastic container with holes drilled throughout the sides, however, there are many more holes and they are drilled on all six sides, evenly spaced. These fruiting chambers are preferable for mushrooms which are grown out of bags, like that of oysters, shiitake, or lion's mane. A layer of moist perlite is placed across the bottom in order to retain moisture, and the grow bag is placed on top of the perlite to fruit. This type of fruiting chamber is also used in the PF Tek method, and there are instructions in the next chapter on how to make one.

Martha fruiting chambers are essentially miniature indoor greenhouses. They are a small-scale structure that is composed of shelves and encased by a plastic cover which has a zipper enclosure to allow entry. There are plenty of resources online for how to make one of these, but know they are a bit more complicated and effortful than the tub chambers above. For that reason, it's recommended that you use a fruiting monotub or shotgun fruiting chamber at first.

There are 4 main variables that need to be considered and maintained when you are fruiting indoors. These are humidity, temperature, lighting, and fresh air exchange.

1. **Humidity:** Ensure you are misting regularly, however only when you see the surface drying

up. Mushrooms need to be hydrated. You should be able to see tiny water droplets on the surface of your mycelium, however, not too much. If you see pools of water forming on the surface, simply dab with a paper towel to soak up excess water, and don't mist again until necessary. You can also purchase a reptile fogger which is just a mini humidifier that you can run inside your fruiting chamber for an hour a day.

2. **Temperature:** Depending on the species that you are growing, the temperature requirements may vary, however, generally the range is from 60-70 °F (15-21°C). Keep a temperature gauge nearby so that you know what you're working with. You can play around with how you control temperature. If you have a designated growing room, you can use a mini air conditioner or space heater to maintain the necessary temperatures. Otherwise, try to fruit your mushrooms in an area of your house that you know generally sits around the required temperature.

3. **Lighting:** Mushrooms need light in order to stimulate growth, but not in the same way as plants. Plants need sunlight for photosynthesis, but mushrooms just use light as a signal that it's time to fruit. That being said, you need to place your mushrooms in an

area that has indirect sunlight, similar to how they might receive light in the woods with trees overhead and light peaking through at certain hours of the day. This can be inside in rooms with windows, or outside in partially shaded areas. However, if growing in a room without windows, for example in a garage, you can use an LED light on a timer to stimulate growth by simulating circadian rhythms through a 12-hour-on/12-hour-off cycle.

4. **Fresh air exchange:** Fanning your fruiting chamber (tub, container) is also a must to allow for fresh air exchange. Mushrooms are like animals in the sense that they breathe in oxygen and breath out carbon dioxide. It's important to give them enough fresh air to get the necessary oxygen, while also allowing the carbon dioxide to exit the fruiting chamber and prevent any buildup. A couple of times per day should suffice to increase fresh air exchange. For obvious reasons, this can't be isn't as necessary with grow bags that are not in a fruiting chamber.

5

MAKING YOUR OWN SPAWN

*P*remade spawn is a great way to get started when growing mushrooms. It's generally easy to obtain, and you don't have to have any equipment, and it saves a lot of time and effort while you're still learning how to grow. However, many growers will eventually get to a point where they want to try making their own spawn. Some benefits of creating your own spawn include cost effectiveness, allowing you to have more control over the types of mushroom you can grow, and it also teaches you a lot about mycelial growth. Not to mention, it's quite satisfying and rewarding to start a grow from your very own batch of spawn!

There are many different ways that you can create your own mushroom spawn ranging from easier low tech methods to high tech methods needing more equipment. In this chapter we'll go over several different methods for making grain spawn at home. We'll start out with the easier methods, and finish with a couple methods that require a bit more effort and equipment, but can still be done at home if you choose to do so. That being said, let's get spawning!

STEM BUTT METHOD

The stem butt method is by far the easiest and most convenient way to make your own spawn. This method provides a way to cultivate mushrooms with no equipment, and hardly any time or effort. All you need is cardboard, stem butts, and a container (preferably an airtight sealable container). Stem butts are just the very bottom of the mushroom stem that physically connects into the ground and has mycelium on it. You can take these stem butts, and when fresh, the mycelium will grow onto a substrate which can then be expanded and used as spawn.

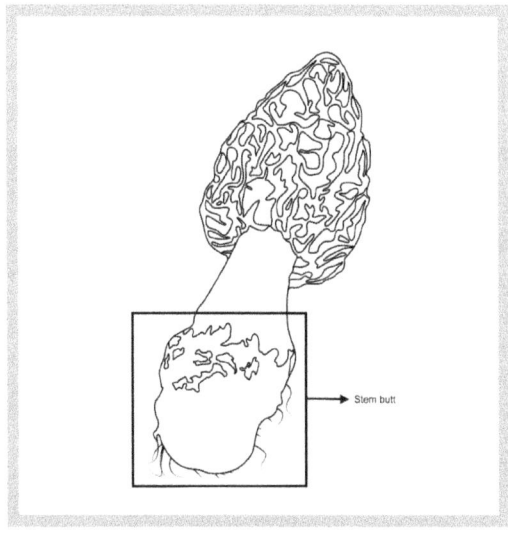

Stem butt of Morel mushroom.

Whether you're foraging or picking mushrooms from a patch you already have in your garden, you'll want to be careful when pulling up the mushrooms to ensure you get the full stem butt out of the ground–you want the root with the hair-like growth still attached to it and intact. Not all mushrooms have this type of root structure called a rhizomorph, but many different mushrooms that do have rhizomorphs can grow surprisingly well from their stem butts. This method is known to work particularly well for Oysters, Piopinnis, Turkey Tails, and Morels (if you're lucky enough to have these growing somewhere near you), but for this example I'll be using Oysters.

. . .

For the Stem Butt method you will need:

- Freshly picked and cut stem butts from Oysters
- Cardboard (Plain corrugated cardboard with no ink. Mushrooms are will absorb the chemicals in the ink which can obviously be detrimental to your spawn growth)
- A large plastic tub or bucket
- Plastic tupperware container with a sealable lid

Method:

1. Shred the cardboard into small 1 inch pieces by cutting with scissors, or ripping by hand.
2. Place the cardboard in a large plastic tub or bucket.
3. Pour the boiling water over the shredded cardboard. This process will hydrate the cardboard and kill off other microorganisms. It won't be 100% effective at killing off everything but it will be good enough. Cover your plastic tub with a cover and leave the cardboard to soak for around an hour.
4. Once the cardboard cools down, drain and set it aside.
5. Get your plastic container and poke some small holes in the sides for ventilation (around 8-12 will do). *Top Tip- to poke the right sized holes without cracking the container, I heat up a nail

using a lighter which will easily go through the
plastic.

6. Ring out some of the excess moisture in the
    cardboard with your hands then layer it on the
    bottom of the container. Fill up ¼ of the
    container.

7. Now add the stem butts on top of the
    cardboard. The more the merrier, be generous,
    as the more you use the more chance the
    mycelium has to take hold.

8. Add another layer of cardboard on top of the
    stem butts and keep on adding layers of stem
    butts and cardboard until the container is
    filled. Once you have completed this, seal the
    lid of the container.

9. You have almost completed the process—you
    now simply need to wait for a couple of weeks
    for the mycelium to do its thing and colonize
    the cardboard. The container should be placed
    in a dark room with a warm temperature. Wait
    for the substrate to become fully colonized.
    Remember to resist the urge to open the lid
    during the colonization period. This of course
    leads to an increased chance of molds or other
    fungi entering the container and
    contaminating your batch.

10. Once you see the spawn completely colonized
    with the mycelium having fully taken hold, it's
    ready to use as your spawn. You can now use

this in any of the other methods explained in chapter 4.

11. Your spawn will keep for around 2 weeks.

Using the stem butt method is a great, cheap, and easy way to create your own spawn, especially if you're looking for something quick and low-tech. However, it can be less reliable than other methods that require a more sterile process and a bit more equipment. It is a fun method to try nonetheless, but if you are ok with spending more time and getting a few more pieces of equipment, the next method is another great way to make spawn at home. It's called the PF Tek method.

PF TEK METHOD

This method was originally created by Robert Mcpherson, also known as Psilocybe Fanaticus (PF). It became famous because it is generally cheap and beginner-friendly. It can be used to grow several types of mushrooms including oyster mushrooms and lion's mane. PF Tek does require a few more materials, but doesn't require a ton of expensive equipment other than a pressure cooker, which can even be replaced with a large pot. Of course, if you do have access to a pressure cooker, these are always best practice because they can help you achieve complete sterilization. However, the cool thing about PF Tek is that complete sterilization is not necessary to get good results. Additionally, this method will take you from creating your spawn straight into fruiting.

Here's what you'll need:

- ½ pint mason jars
- Brown rice flour
- Vermiculite
- Spoon/spatula for mixing
- Large mixing bowl/container
- Pressure cooker or a large pot
- Source of heat to act as a sterilizer (i.e. alcohol lamp, lighter, butane torch)
- Water

- Isopropyl alcohol for cleaning
- Aluminium foil
- Spore syringe (can be purchased online)
- Misting bottle
- Drill or hammer and nail to poke holes in the lid
- Still air box
- Shotgun fruiting chamber

Brown rice flour mixed with vermiculite acts as the substrate for this method, which is later placed in glass mason jars, and sterilized. These will be your brown rice flour cakes (BRF cakes) which are eventually inoculated with your liquid spore syringe. You can get brown rice flour from your local grocery store usually, but if you can't find any, you can always look online or just blend up some brown rice in a food processor to create flour. Vermiculite is often used to aerate garden soil, so it can typically be found at gardening centers. For PF Tek, it serves a similar purpose in that it provides space throughout the brown rice flour for the mycelium to colonize, while the rice flour itself provides the actual nutrition.

Lastly, if you don't have a still air box or a shotgun fruiting chamber, they are really easy to make. A still air box is essentially just a large, clear plastic tote/storage box with two holes cut out for your arms, and a shotgun fruiting chamber is the same type of box but with small holes drilled evenly all over the box. At the end of the chapter, there will be instructions on how to make both.

Method:

1. Start off by drilling 3 or 4 evenly spaced holes around the perimeter of the lid by using a 3mm drill bit. You can also use 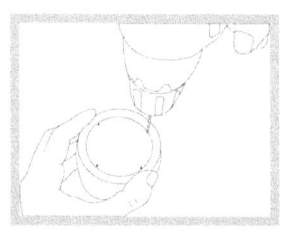 a hammer and a nail if you don't have a drill, but make sure the holes are not larger than 2-3mm. This is where you will be injecting the spores using the syringe.

2. Disinfect the jars by wiping them down with alcohol.

3. Now you'll need to mix the substrate in a large bowl. Mix 6 cups of vermiculite with 3 cups of water thoroughly. Add 3 cups of brown rice flour to this mixture and again mix well, so there aren't any clumps of the brown rice flour and everything is evenly distributed. This mixture should be enough for roughly 12 glass jars.

4. Fill each jar with the substrate mixture but leave about half an inch of space at the top of the jar. You don't want to pack the substrate

down too tightly, but you can tap on the bottom of them to help compact them slightly. Wipe down the inside neck of the jar with a clean paper towel, and top it off with a layer of dry vermiculite to the top of the jar–this acts as a barrier and helps to lessen chances of contamination when injecting the spores.

5. Cover the jars with the lids and screw them tightly and place masking tape over the holes that have been drilled or poked into the lid. Then place a small sheet of tin foil over each jar and fold it over the edge of the lid. This helps to ensure that liquid does not enter the jars during sterilization.

6. Now you need to sterilize the jars. The jars will need to be steamed in a large pot on the stove. Place a small metal rack or some mason jar lids at the bottom of the pot to give your jars a base, and prevent them from directly touching the pot. Fill the bottom of the pot with an inch or so of water. Place the jars on the rack and cover the pot, and leave the jars steaming for roughly 1.5 hours. You can always add more water to the bottom if you notice the water level has gone down too much. If you are using a pressure cooker, you'll still want to line the bottom with a rack or lids, but you only have to sterilize the jars for 45 minutes starting from when the cooker has reached 15psi.

7. Once the jars are sterilized, leave them inside the pot to cool down and do not open the lid of the pot till the jars are ready for inoculation. If you used a pressure cooker, release the pressure as instructed by the manufacturer and then let the jars cool. Make sure your jars are at room temperature before moving on to the next step. I usually just leave my jars to cool overnight, and continue in the morning.

8. After the jars have cooled, you can remove the tin foil. You are going to want to inoculate inside your still air box. Wipe down all your materials and utensils with alcohol, including the air box and the outside/lids of the jars, then place them into the still air box. Once you have everything you need for inoculation in the still air box (jars, flame source, spore syringe), you can begin the inoculation process.

9. Give the syringe a good shake before using it to evenly distribute the spores present inside. After removing the plastic cover from the needle, sterilize it with your flame source. Flame the needle outside of the still air box, to the point where you can see it turning red, then take it back into the still air box. Pull the tape back that you had covered the holes on the lid with and start injecting the spore liquid as evenly as possible through the holes you've drilled in the lids. You don't need a ton of

liquid per hole (in theory, you only need around 0.5ml per hole, but this is much easier said than done, so just do your best). Cover the holes again with the tape once the injections are done, and repeat the process for each jar. Don't forget to flame the needle before each new jar.

10. For the incubation period the jars should be placed in a warm and dry place with no light. This will accelerate colonization. If you want to maintain the temperature it should be somewhere around 75-84°F (24-29°C). Full colonization normally takes around 2 -3 three weeks to completely fill the jars with mycelium. Be mindful of any other growth inside the jars and keep observing them. If you see any contamination, the jar should be discarded right away.

11. Once they have been fully colonized, and as long as you can see that the mycelium has fully covered the substrate, it's time to fruit! Now you can take the cakes out of the jars and soak them in cold water for about 24 hours. Put them in a large bowl or container that is deep enough to submerge them fully. They will want to float, so place something on top of them like a plate or bowl to hold them down. This simply rehydrates the cakes for fruiting.

12. Now that the cakes are nice and hydrated,

you'll want to place them into a shotgun fruiting chamber. Place each cake on top of a small square of tin foil that is just larger than the BRF cakes. Spray them down multiple times a day and fan them with the lid before replacing it to make sure they are getting enough fresh air.

With this method, you can also use the BRF cakes as spawn–simply break them up and inoculate them evenly into a larger fruiting substrate like the coco coir and vermiculite mix in a large plastic tub, to get a larger yield.

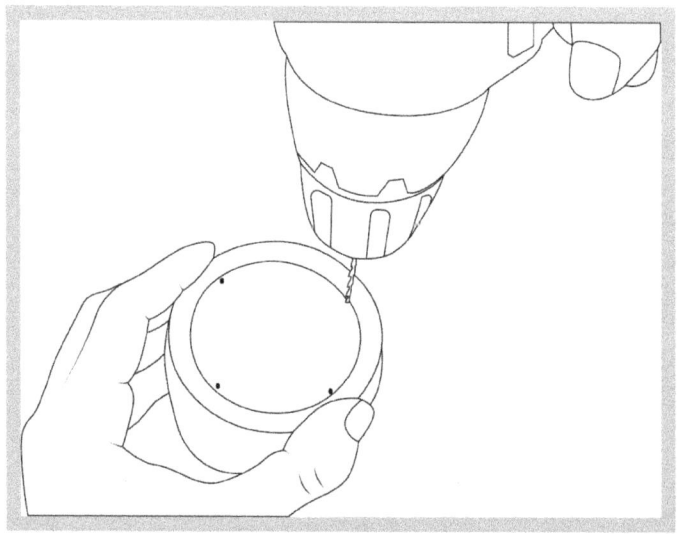

Drilling holes in lid of mason jar (Step 1)

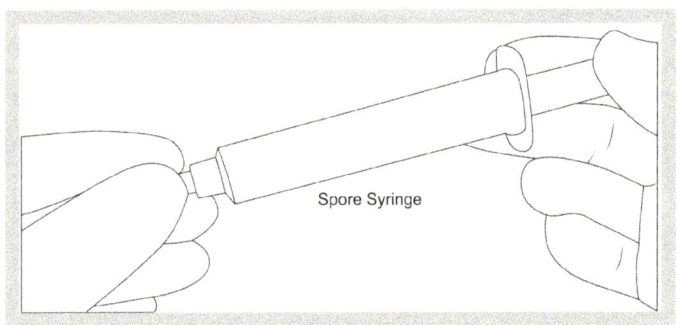

Spore syringe containing liquid spores or liquid mycelium

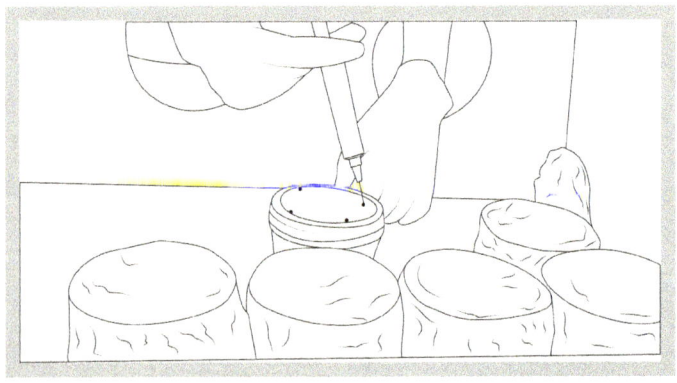

Inoculation of BRF cakes using the spore syringe (Step 8)

Soaking of BRF cakes in water. Don't forget to place plate on top to submerge (Step 10)

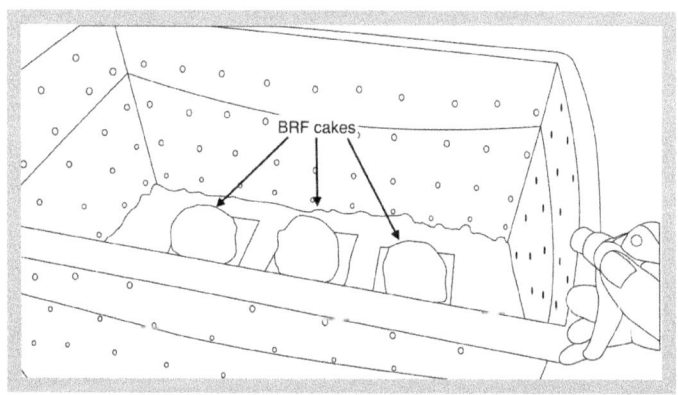

BRF cakes placed on tin foil squares ready for fruiting in a shotgun fruiting chamber (Step 11)

HOW TO MAKE YOUR OWN GRAIN SPAWN USING A SILICONE INJECTION PORT

Another great method of generating your own grain spawn is similar to that of the PF Tek method. However, it is designed to be used as a spawn to directly add to a bulk substrate rather than being used to fruit mushrooms on its own. This method will produce a greater volume of grain spawn than the PF Tek method. Additionally, this method allows you to inoculate your grains with your spore syringe without having to use a still air box or laminar flow hood.

To make 5 mason jars (17oz each) of spawn, you will need:

- A cereal grain (rye, wheat berries, oat berries, brown rice, corn etc.). You'll need 1.5 full jars of dry grain (it will expand to around 3.5 times the dry weight due to absorption of the water).
- Mason jars with regular screw caps (17oz)
- Drill with ¼ and ⅛ inch drill bit
- High temperature silicone sealing agent (*Don't use a regular silicone sealing agent as it will melt during the sterilization process)
- Bucket with water (for soaking your grain)
- Pan (And a stove for heating)
- 10 ml Spore syringe with inoculated liquid culture. (I use Beacon Hill Mushrooms with

great success (UK). I have friends in the US who use Mycelium Emporium who come highly recommended)
- Autoclave/pressure cooker
- Colander/sieve

Method:

1. Measure out your spawning substrate by filling up 1 and a half mason jars with your grain of choice.
2. Soak your grain in a bucket of water for 12 hours. Ensure all your grain is fully submerged. The purpose of this step is to hydrate your grain which will allow for better colonisation of the mycelium. *Don't soak for much longer than 12 hours as you want your grains to be hydrated but not to sprout.
3. While your grain spawn is soaking, drill two holes in the lids of the mason jar tops. Drill a larger ¼ inch hole in the centre of the cap, and a small ⅛ inch hole which will be the inoculation port.
4. The larger ¼ inch hole needs filling with pillow stuffing by simply pulling through a small chunk so it's evenly spread through both sides of the jar cap. This is to allow the mycelium to breathe while reducing the chance for contaminants getting through to the grain.

5. The smaller ⅛ inch hole needs filling with a small dab of high temperature silicone sealant and left to dry. This will create a self healing injection port, meaning when you put the needle through it to inoculate your mycelium and pull the needle out again it will close up immediately ensuring sterile conditions are maintained inside the jar.

6. Next, transfer the grains from the bucket to your pan and heat on a low heat for 15 minutes. This will allow the grains to become fully hydrated. (Don't heat for too long or at too high of a temperature as this will cause the grain to split open and make it more difficult for the mycelium to take hold).

7. After 15 minutes, drain your grains in a colander/sieve and leave to dry for between 60-90 minutes.

8. Fill your mason jars with the grain, but leave about a 1-2 inch gap at the top. Screw the cap on and then wrap a layer of kitchen foil over the top of the lid. This is to prevent any condensation dripping back through the pillow stuffing during sterilization.

9. Place your jars into your pressure cooker/autoclave and sterilize your jars for 90 minutes at a PSI of 15. The 90 minutes starts when the PSI reaches 15, not when you initially start it.

10. After 90 minutes take the jars outs of the pressure cooker and leave to cool until room temperature. Your jars are now ready to inoculate with mycelium.

11. Take your sterile needle syringe and insert the needle through your self healing injection port and inject 2ml into your grain. Repeat the process for all 5 jars.

12. Leave your jars in a dry place such as a cupboard for a couple of weeks until your grains have become fully colonized. Once they are fully colonized, they are ready to use to inoculate your fruiting substrate!

Quart mason jars with tin foil over the top, ready to be sterilized in the pressure cooker

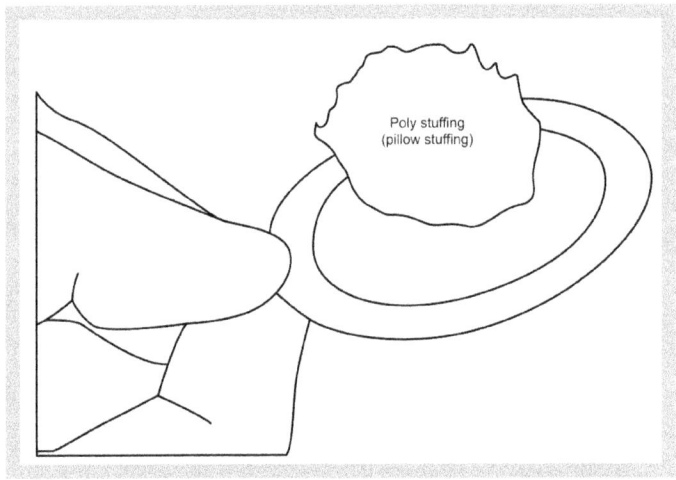

Poly stuffing fitted into drilled out hole in the center of the lid

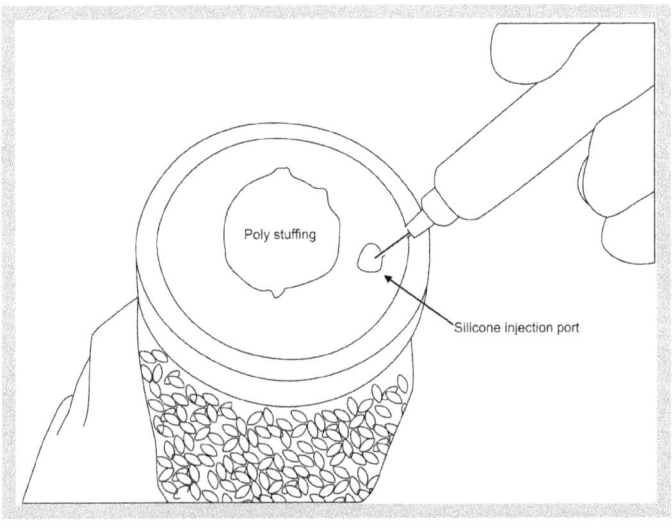

Injection of liquid spores into sterilised grain through self-healing injection port

HOW TO MAKE A STILL AIRBOX

A still air box is a useful piece of low tech equipment which can be used to ensure that your work environment is clean and hygienic, without the need for more expensive equipment such as a laminar flow hood. It creates an environment where there is minimal air movement and no drafts that may cause contaminants to enter your work space.

To make a still air box you will need:

- A big clear plastic storage box with a volume of between 80-110 litres.
- A metal tin with a diameter of 5-6 inches.
- A hob or stovetop for heating up the tins
- Oven safe gloves
- A sharpie or other marker

Method:

1. Use the marker pen and tin to mark where the holes will be by placing the tin on the box. You want them halfway up from the bottom of the box to the top with a distance of between 8-10 inches from edge to edge of each circle.
2. Once you are happy with the placement of the holes. Place the metal tin on the hob. Make sure there is no paper or other material on the

metal tin as we don't want there to be any burning. Having said that, you will be melting plastic using this tin, so open any nearby windows and doors to let fresh air flow inside.

3. Heat the tin until it starts turning red hot. With your oven gloves, carefully pick up the metal tin and gently place it on the hole that you have previously marked out. Gently press the tin downwards to melt the hole out.

4. The tin should fairly easily go through the plastic and you should have your first hole completed. The plastic from the container will most likely harden on the inside of the tin, so just remove it and pop it out once it has cooled.

5. Repeat the process for the second hole. Make sure there is no plastic left on the tin from the first hole, as you don't want to be burning plastic on the stove.

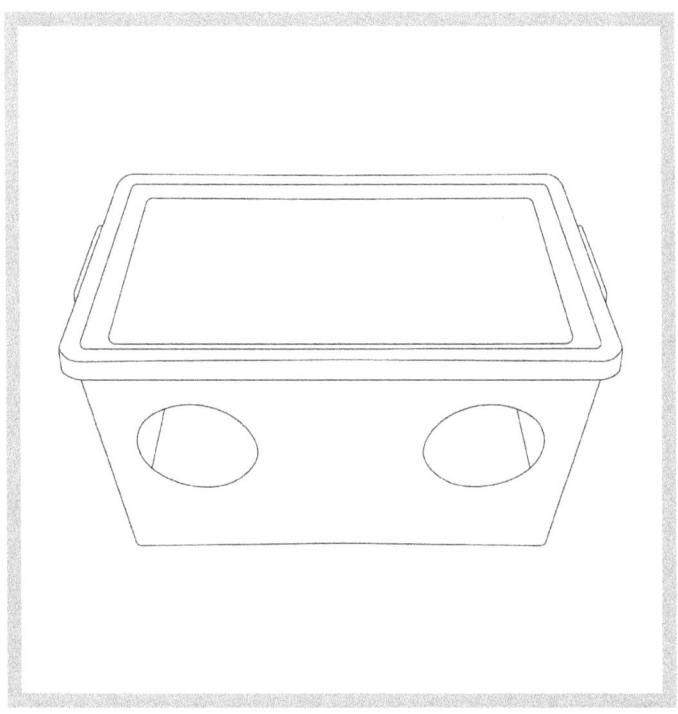

Still air box finished product (when actually using the still air box, it will be turned upside down so the larger surface area is on the bottom).

Some things to note while making your still air box:

- Make sure to have a few windows open to allow fresh air in, as you will be melting plastic and likely causing a few fumes to rise up.
- Have a place ready, like a nearby sink, to put the hot tin in once you are done with it.
- Ensure the box is in a position where you won't need to move it around while you are melting the holes out.

HOW TO MAKE A SHOTGUN FRUITING CHAMBER

Shotgun fruiting chambers are very simple to make, and can be done with pretty common tools. These chambers help to provide more constant conditions for our mushrooms by helping to maintain humidity levels and allowing for fresh air. Many people just starting out who are growing using grow kits use them to create a more optimal environment for the grow kit. They are also used for fruiting blocks in grow bags. All a shotgun fruiting chamber is, is a large clear plastic tote, similar to the one used for the still air box, with small holes drilled evenly around the box, and a thick layer of moist perlite layered across the bottom. The perlite serves the purpose of maintaining constant moisture levels.

Here's what you'll need:

- Large clear plastic tote
- Drill with ¼ inch drill bit
- Perlite (coarse)
- Measuring tape
- Sharpie

The first step in creating the fruiting chamber is to mark out evenly spaced holes all around the box to create even air flow. Take your measuring tape and mark out a grid of holes that are spaced 2 inches apart. You want holes on all 6 sides of the box, including the top and bottom.

Now, you're simply going to drill out each hole that you've marked out, with your ¼ inch drill bit. Be careful not to push too hard with the drill, because this could cause the plastic to split. This step will feel a bit tedious, but it's the only step that takes much effort for this process.

Once the holes have been drilled, it's time to fill the bottom with perlite. You want to make sure you're using coarse perlite, not fine, so that it retains water better and also so that it doesn't fall through the bottom holes as much. Fill the bottom with an even layer all the way across, around 3-4 inches thick.

Add water to the perlite and mix it around thoroughly. You want the perlite to be nice and moist, but not so wet that there is a flow of water coming out of the bottom of the fruiting chamber. Once you're done with that, you're ready to add your mushroom fruiting blocks or grow kits in! Make sure that you fan it with the lid and mist it at least 2 times a day, but 3 or 4 is better if possible.

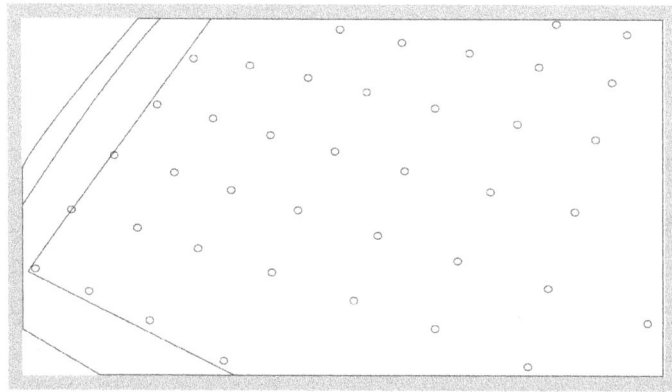

Drilled holes spaced evenly apart

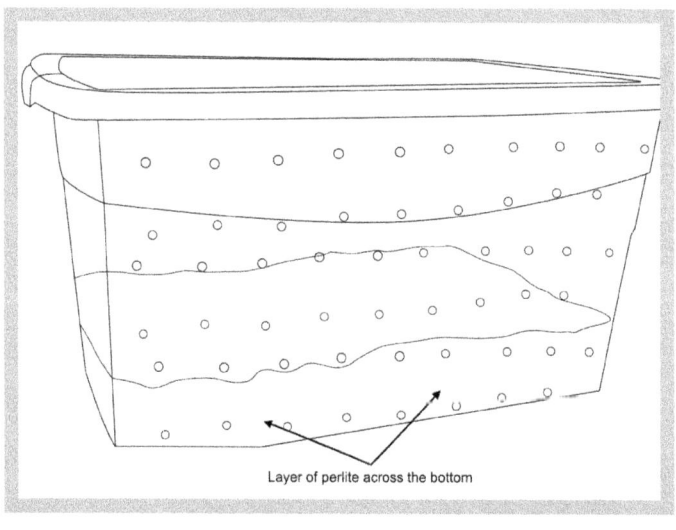

Layer of perlite across the bottom

Shotgun fruiting chamber layered with perlite

FROM SPORE TO SPAWN

HOW TO MAKE SPORE PRINTS

What is a spore print? A spore print is a powdery deposit of mushroom spores which are obtained by allowing the spore of the fruiting body to fall onto a surface underneath.

Why would we take a spore print? The spores obtained using a spore printing collection method can be transferred to an agar solution and mycelium can be grown from this which in turn can be transferred to a grain or other substrate to make your own spawn.

To make spore prints you will need:

- A few fresh mushroom caps
- Kitchen foil
- Sterile gloves
- Sterile cutting device- scissors, knife etc.
- Baking dish
- Pipette

Method:

1. Cover the bottom of your baking tray with a line of kitchen foil.

2. Cut off the cap of your mushrooms with the sterile cutting instrument.

3. Place the mushroom cap gills and spore side down onto the kitchen foil.

4. Fill the pipette up with water and drop a couple of droplets on the top of the mushroom cap. This mimics rainfall in the wild and stimulates the mushrooms to disperse their spores. Do not drip too much water on the tops of the caps as this could cause too much water to drip down onto the foil.

5. Cover the top of the baking dish with a layer of foil and make sure it's tightly folded round the sides. Leave for two days at room temperature.

6. After 2 days the mushroom caps will have left their mark. Take off the cover and remove the mushroom caps. You should be left with a spore sprint which will be black or brown in colour.

HOW TO TRANSFER A SPORE PRINT TO AGAR

With your spore prints complete, we can now transfer them onto agar which in turn will be used to grow the mycelium. The method is pretty simple and only requires a few steps.

What is agar? Agar is a jelly like substance which is commonly used in laboratory settings for growing bacteria , moulds and obviously fungi. It serves as a great nutritious source for fungi allowing a fairly rapid growth once it takes hold.

Where you can source agar? You can buy agar dishes from Amazon or various places online. Make sure you buy the petri dishes with the agar already inside, because having to make your own agar and filling up the dishes yourself can be rather effortful.

What you will need for this method:

- Spore print
- A blade
- Still air box
- Agar dish
- Flame source
- Gloves
- Face mask

Method:

1. Place everything that you need for this process from the list above apart from the blade and flame source into your still air box.
2. Undo the lids of your agar dishes, however do not completely open the lids. The lids need to be opened for as little time as possible to limit the chance of contaminants reaching the agar and contaminating your dish

3. Sterilize your blade with your flame source, and heat it until it's red hot. Do this outside of the box to prevent contamination.

4. Once this is done, inside the still air box open up your spore print, being careful not to touch the spore directly with your glove. Place the spore print down again with the spore print facing up, ready to use.

5. Now is time to open up your agar dish. Take the lid off the agar dish

6. Pick up your kitchen foil with the spore print on it, and with the blade, scrape off a few small specs of the black spores over the dish and scrape them onto the agar. You don't need to scrape off much, just enough that you can see a few specs of black on the agar. This will be enough to colonize the agar. Limit the amount of time the agar is exposed to the air, so as soon as you have your spores on the agar close the lid of the petri dish

7. Repeat the process with as many dishes as you want to do. I usually do 3-5 at a time.

8. After 1-2 weeks your agar should be colonized with the mycelium.

MAKING TRANSFERS ON AGAR

As sterile as your process may have been when carrying out the spore prints there is a chance that your agar dish may show signs of contamination even if there is some healthy growth of mycelium. This would in turn lead to your grain spawn becoming contaminated when we transfer the agar into the grain. For this reason it is recommended that you do at least one transfer from your agar dish to a fresh agar dish.

Top two signs of contamination on the agar:

- Slime is one of the main signs that your petri dish is contaminated. This usually indicates that there is some form of bacterial growth.
- Any color that is not the white mycelium growth.

For agar to agar transfer you need:

- Agar with mycelium growth
- Fresh agar dish
- Blade
- Heat source

Method:

1. Sterilize your blade using the heat source, again making sure the blade is red hot.
2. Undo the lids without taking them off fully, on both agar dishes.
3. With your blade make a cut into the mycelium

roughly 1 cm thickness and lift out the cut of mycelium and transfer to the fresh agar plate, remembering to have the lid open for as little time as possible.

4. Pop the lid back onto the new agar plate and allow the mycelium to do what mycelium does best. Some people do multiple transfers to ensure a non-contaminated culture. I usually do just one and then inspect to see if there is any contamination before transferring to the grain.

GENERATING SPAWN FROM YOUR AGAR CULTURE

The last step which will have taken you from spores to spawn, is achieved by transferring your agar culture to your ready and waiting sterilized grain or sawdust substrate. Once you are happy with your mycelium culture on the agar dish meaning it has fully colonised the agar and most importantly there is no contamination, then we can complete this final step. After successfully transferring your agar culture to sterilized grain it will quickly take hold on the grain and become ready to use as spawn.

What you will need:

- Your mycelium agar dishes

- Sterilized grain spawn in a mason jar
- Alcohol wipes (not essential)
- A blade
- Heat source
- Still air box

Method:

1. Before thinking about the transfer from agar to grain/sawdust, you first of all need to fully sterilize your jar(s) of grain or sawdust in your pressure cooker or autoclave. You should know how to do this by now.
2. Once sterilized you should have everything you need inside your still air box.
3. Heat the blade to sterilize it outside of the still air box and then place it back inside your still airbag ready to use.
4. Loosen the lids or your jars. (For these mason jars you need to drill one hole in the centre ¼ inch and put pillow stuffing in the hole. Again cover with kitchen foil when sterilizing).
5. Open your agar dish and with your blade score the agar 5 lines straight down the agar and 5 lines straight across. This helps to break up the agar so it can be more evenly dispersed throughout the grain or sawdust for a quick colonisation.
6. Simply, open your mason jar lid and tip the

agar and mycelium into the jar and quickly return the lid and screw tightly.

7. Give the jar a really good shake to evenly distribute the mycelium.

8. Place in a dark room and allow colonization. After 1-2 weeks you should see that the grain or sawdust has been fully colonized and it is then ready to add to your fruiting substrate.

CLONING MUSHROOMS TO PRODUCE SPAWN

What is mushroom cloning? Cloning is the process of taking tissue from the live fruiting body of a mushroom stem, and transferring it to an agar culture where it will grow and expand.

Why is cloning important? There are two reasons. First, this method will produce genetically identical mushrooms, whereas using spore prints will have some variations. Therefore, this is a great technique if you want to produce identical mushrooms with superior genetics. Second, you can skip the process of generating mycelium from spores which will save you about 1-2 weeks in time.

Which mushrooms can I use for cloning? You can use any mushrooms; those you have grown from home, foraged mushrooms, and even grocery store bought mushrooms. However, this can only be done with freshly harvested mushrooms, as in those which have been dehydrated, their mycelium will have died and it would be nearly impossible to bring it back to life.

What you will need:

- A freshly picked mushroom with a large, healthy stem
- Blade
- Heat source

- Agar dishes
- Still air box
- Gloves

Method:

1. Undo the agar dishes without fully opening them.
2. Using your hands, split the mushroom stem open, revealing the fleshy body of the stem. This step is to expose a part of the stem which hasn't been in contact with the air which might have contaminants.
3. With your blade carve out roughly a 1cm square part of the stem.
4. Take off the lid of the agar dish and transfer the piece of stem you have just cut out to the agar dish. Close the lid and wait for the mycelium to colonise.
5. Two weeks later your mycelium will be ready to transfer to your grain or sawdust to generate spawn using the same aforementioned method from the last section.

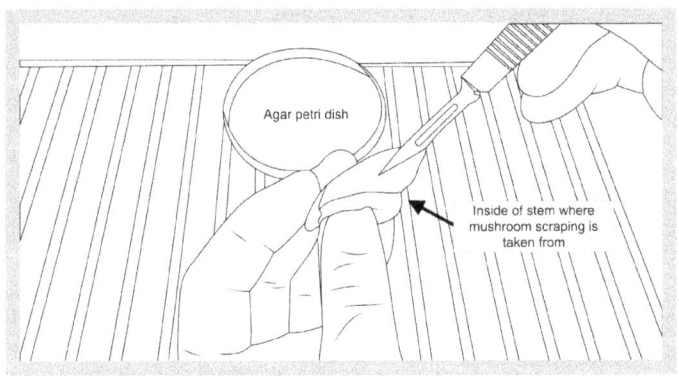

Transfer of flesh from inside of stem onto an agar petri dish

When cloning you will likely not need to make transfers between agar plates as you would have to when making spore prints. The reason for this is that there is less likely to be contamination when cloning due to the chance of contamination for spore prints generally coming from the kitchen foil. Having said that, you know the top two signs of contamination to look out for. If you see any of these signs, then perform an agar transfer until you are happy with the mycelium culture you have. Once you are happy, you can then easily transfer to a grain as detailed in the previous method.

6

OUTDOOR GROWING

*G*rowing mushrooms outdoors is becoming an increasingly common site in many gardens. Outdoor mushroom cultivation can be a fun alternative to growing indoors, one that comes with its unique set of challenges. There are 3 main ways that I have used to grow mushrooms outdoors in the past and they are growing on logs, creating a mushroom bed, and growing mushrooms in a polytunnel.

GROWING ON LOGS

Logs You Can Inoculate

The first thing you need to establish before you start thinking about growing from plug spawn, is the type of log you want to choose. A freshly cut dry hardwood log (Birch, Alder, Oak) is needed and one which is thick enough so that you can drill several holes into it without it snapping. Generally a log about 4ft long and 6 inches in diameter should suffice. Having a freshly cut log is important, as a log that is already dead may have succumbed to wild fungi or moulds, leaving no room for your fungi to take hold and no nutrition that it could survive on.

How to Prep Your Log:

I will always scrub off any lichen before inoculation. Mushrooms can cohabitate with the lichen, however, it is another microorganism that can compete with your mushrooms, so best to remove it before starting. I use a steel brush to scrub the unwanted competitors off, but not too hard, as we want to preserve the outer bark.

How to Inoculate Your Logs:

When your plug spawn arrives, with clean hands count how many there are as that is the number of holes you will need to drill. Find the log or a few logs that you have chosen to inoculate with the wooden dowels and drill roughly 1 inch deep holes with 5/16" drill bit. This is usually the size that will allow the dowels to fit snugly in, but of course, drill one hole and check to see if it is a good fit. Then with a hammer, knock in your mycelium inoculated wooden dowels in. In terms of spacing, 2-4 inches between each dowel is recommended, so you'll have around 50 holes in a 4 foot long log.

Sealing Your Log:

There is one final step which is often forgotten about when inoculating logs and that is to 'seal' the ends of the logs. Either end of your log and the individual dowels need sealing, this is most often done with melted beeswax or paraffin. Simply get a new, clean paint brush and coat both ends of your log with a layer of either substance as well as the top of each individual dowel insertion. The reason for this is to keep other organisms out from entering the log and providing unwanted competition–this is the same reason why leaving the bark on is important, to prevent competition.

Where to Keep Your Inoculated Log

So now that you have your log inoculated, what do you do with it? Now you need to consider two variables; sunlight and moisture. Firstly, it is best to place your log on a pallet where it is not in direct contact with the ground, but if you do not have a pallet then a plastic sheet will do just fine. Don't place the log in direct sunlight as the majority of mushroom species will dry out with too much sun which can affect the size and shape. The best place for them would be a shady patch in your garden. Next, you need to consider how much moisture your mushrooms will be getting. If you live in dry arid conditions you will need to be lightly watering your mushrooms most days to make sure they are sufficiently hydrated. With these two important factors addressed all you can do now is sit back and enjoy watching your mushrooms grow. This can take anywhere between 3 months to a couple of years depending on the type of mushrooms you're growing. Mushrooms tend to grow slower outdoors compared to indoors, due to conditions being much more similar to that of their natural environment. However, logs can provide you with flushes for several years after inoculation.

CREATING MUSHROOM BEDS

Growing gourmet mushrooms in outdoor beds is an easy and inexpensive way to grow at home without the hassle of equipment. It's not quite as demanding as growing indoors or on logs. They are quick to put together, and you can often even enjoy a mushroom crop within the same season of inoculating your spawn. Most commonly wine caps and oysters are grown in beds.

If you plan on cultivating in an outdoor bed, all you'll need is your mushroom spawn, straw and wood chips, or compost/manure depending on the type of mushroom you're attempting to grow. A common technique for garden beds is mulching, and if you're acquainted with gardening, you've likely heard of the layering method, which is what I'll be going through now. Mulching brings quite a few benefits to your garden bed such as improving the soil quality by increasing organic matter, retaining water, and also providing a barrier over the soil for edible crops.

Growing Wine Caps in a Garden Bed

For the first example, I thought it would be best to go over one of the easiest types of mushrooms to grow in outdoor beds–the Wine Cap mushroom, or *Stropharia rugosoannulata*. The fact that it's highly unlikely that you'll find these at your local supermarket, and that they can thrive in a variety of conditions, are a couple reasons why this type of mushroom is so appealing to home-growers. Not to mention, their caps can grow up to the size of a frisbee!

Before any inoculation, you'll want to lay the groundwork for your bed (pun intended). Choose a site in your garden that is shade-heavy. Wine caps can do okay in small bouts of direct sunlight, but it's better to keep them somewhere they will be shaded throughout the majority of the day. Clean out any unwanted plants or waste, so that you have a bare ground to work with. Once you have a clean, level surface, lay flat pieces of cardboard down. This step is optional, but it does help with retaining a base layer of moisture, and also suppressing new weeds from growing. Make sure it's plain brown cardboard, not covered in plastic tape or dyes. Now you're ready to mulch, and inoculate.

You'll want to use hardwood for these wood chips, and if you'd like and are able to source it, you can even mix your wood chips with saw dust or chopped up straw. Remove any branches or very large pieces of wood. For an area of roughly 16-20 square feet, you'll need a bag of spawn weighing around 6-8lbs.

Method:

1. Line the base of the bed with an even 1-2 inch layer of wood chips over the cardboard that

you have placed (or the soil if you have not used cardboard).

2. Break up the spawn, and spread an even layer over the wood chips, making sure to avoid leaving any large clumps of spawn in any one place.

3. Add another 1-2 inch layer of wood chips over the spawn.

4. Continue to layer the substrate and spawn until you have run out, or until your bed has reached the height you were aiming for.

5. You can now place a layer of straw over the entire bed to help with moisture retention, and act as a protective barrier from any harsh weather conditions.

6. Water the bed thoroughly, and continue to monitor moisture levels. You don't want the bed to be soggy, but moist enough for the fungi to grow. A good rule of thumb is to water it as you would the rest of your garden.

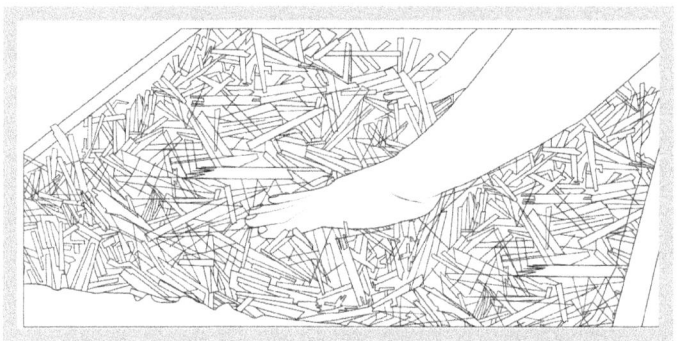

*Place a layer of straw over the lasagna layers of wood chips and
cardboard (Step 5)*

During the first month, it's essential not to let your bed
run dry. This is the time when the mycelium is trying
to establish itself and spread throughout the entire bed,
so it's important to maintain a balanced moisture level.
However, once they are established and have begun to
fruit, they require little maintenance. It can take
anywhere from a few weeks to a few months to see the
initial pins taking form, and this time frame just
depends on the size of your bed, the amount of spawn
you had, and your local climate.

You can use the same method above for Oysters as
well! Instead of using wood chips, you would use
chopped up straw instead, as oysters grow better in less
dense substrates. The same principles apply. Layer the
straw and spawn until you run out, then place a layer
of straw over the top, water thoroughly and continue

to monitor. Oysters like shadier environments, so try to keep them out of direct sunlight.

You can inoculate both Wine Caps and Oysters any time between the spring and fall, as long as it's done with enough time for the mycelium to colonize before temperatures drop below freezing.

GROWING MUSHROOMS IN A POLYTUNNEL

A polytunnel, as the name suggests, is a long tunnel usually made from steel, then covered with the material, polythene. Polythene helps to maintain a controlled environment for the growth of a wide variety of plants and of course we can utilize it to grow mushrooms. You can use both the methods described above (growing on logs and creating mushroom beds), and the polytunnel will just give them more optimal growing conditions.

Where to Locate Your Polytunnel

When growing gourmet mushrooms we need to consider that the environment in which mushrooms and plants grow can be quite different. Mushrooms grow best in woodland conditions with minimal light whereas plants obviously require as much light as possible. For this reason it is recommended that your polytunnel is situated in a part of your garden or allotment which has restricted light, such as under a tree or using a specialist green and white polytunnel cover which restricts light.

Which Mushrooms to Grow in Your Polytunnel

In theory you can grow any mushroom variety in a polytunnel however, you are likely to have more success with some varieties over others. Button, Oysters, Wine Caps, Elm and King Stropharia are all varieties which will grow just fine in a polytunnel.

Maintaining the Environment Inside the Polytunnel

- Water your mushrooms daily using a spray setting on your hose or watering can.
- If it gets too hot in the summer you can open up the polytunnel to let the hot air out. Yes, this can lead to increased chance of contaminants entering, but after a good couple of weeks of colonizing, your mycelium will have hopefully established itself.
- If you'd like, you can also purchase a humidifier to maintain the humidity inside the polytunnel. This can be turned on for an hour, once daily.

7

HARVESTING AND PROCESSING

*A*fter you've put in all the hard work, and your mycelium has given rise to your gourmet mushrooms, all that is left to do is to harvest and process the fruits of your labor! I have already briefly mentioned when to harvest each type of mushroom in the methods previously stated, but here is a simple breakdown of all the mushrooms you may be growing. This is a general guide and of course the time it takes your mushrooms to fruit can vary depending on a number of variables, which I am sure you are familiar with by now.

Oyster Mushrooms

Oyster mushrooms can usually be harvested 3-4 weeks after inoculation or after 1 week after you first see them pinning. I like to harvest them when the cap is still round but starting to flatten. You can wait until the cap has completely flattened.

Shiitake Mushrooms

Shiitake mushrooms will take much longer than the fast growing Oyster varieties. They can take anywhere from 4-9 months to fruit. The best time to harvest them is when the caps are formed but still a little curled under with around 60-80% of the gills exposed. This allows for maximum protection of the gills on the underside of the cap as flattened caps leads to increased chance of the gills bruising. Bruising of the gills shortens the shelf life of shiitakes. However, flat capped shiitake mushrooms often make a better cooking option, so if they're going straight to your frying pan I would let them flatten out.

Maitake Mushrooms

Maitakes, like shiitakes, can take a bit longer than most other varieties of gourmet mushrooms and will take up to 4 months before they are ready to fruit. Fruiting itself can take another month or so.

Lion's Mane

Lion's mane mushrooms are good to harvest when they have a healthy spine development around a ¼ inch in length. There should be a bit of give in it and it should feel squishy. Lions mane when growing indoors should be ready to harvest within a month to 6 weeks. The longer the spines, the further past its prime it is.

Enoki Mushrooms

Enoki mushrooms when grown indoors can usually be ready to harvest after 2-3 months. Ideally you want to harvest them when they have their traditional long stem roughly 4-6 inches in length.

Button Mushrooms

You can expect to harvest your classic button mushrooms after 2-3 months.They are fairly easy to know when to harvest when they have a good healthy stem and large cap as you would expect to see at the grocery store.

HOW TO STORE YOUR MUSHROOMS

Once you have harvested your mushrooms, you then need to think about storage. Fridging, freezing, and drying mushrooms are your 3 options.

Keeping mushrooms in the fridge

If you want to refrigerate the mushrooms, you don't need to wash them until you want to cook them. Simply place them in a sealable bag or container in your fridge. The bag or container will prevent the mushrooms from absorbing any excess moisture, thus preventing them from becoming moldy or soggy. Avoid storing them in the vegetable drawer inside the fridge, since the environment will be too moist for them. Mushrooms act like sponges when it comes to absorbing odors, so avoid placing them next to strong-smelling foods. Treat your mushrooms with care and try not to stack other vegetables on top of them. This will cause them to become de-shaped or bruised.

How long do varieties keep for?

Oysters: 5-7 days

Maitake: 5 days

Shiitakes: 14 days

Lion's Mane: 7 days

Enoki: 14 days

Button: 7 days

How to Freeze Mushrooms

A great way of preserving a large flush of mushrooms is by freezing them. However, they cannot be frozen raw. Mushrooms need to be cooked before they are frozen to minimize enzyme activity and preserve their quality. If you freeze raw mushrooms, the texture will change upon unthawing them and they won't be very good. You want to pick, cook and freeze them as soon after the harvest as you can if you're planning on freezing them, and if possible, avoid waiting until the mushrooms begin to deteriorate. Mushrooms can be frozen within a dish, or by themselves. If you freeze them by themselves, saute them in a pan to allow the moisture to come out, add any seasoning you'd like, then drain the liquid, place them in a freezer bag or container, and you're good to go!

How to Dry Mushrooms

The final great way to store mushrooms is of course to dry them, also known as dehydrating. This elongates their shelf life from 1 week in the fridge to 6-12 months. They can be delicious when used in soups, sauces, stews or eaten on their own. It can be done either with a dehydrator, or in an oven on the lowest heat setting.

The process is really simple. Here's how you do it:

- Slice your mushrooms into your desired thickness (somewhere between ¼-½ inch thick)
- Wash them to remove dirt
- Place on a baking tray and sprinkle with some seasoning (Garlic powder, salt, pepper, sugar are a few options. Whatever flavor you'd like!)
- Put the baking tray in a preheated oven at 50-70 °C (122-178 °F)
- Leave for 2 hours. Then flip so both sides get an even crisp.
- After 4 hours your mushrooms should be nice and crispy and can be stored in a container and eaten within one year.

You can also use a dehydrator. You'll basically just want to slice the mushrooms and place them on the dehydrator in an even layer, without any overlap so that all the pieces have good airflow around them. Place them on medium heat (around 110 °F) until they are crispy. Also refer to the manufacturer instructions when using your dehydrator.

8

SOMETHING'S NOT RIGHT HERE– HOW CAN I FIX IT? PROBLEMS AND SOLUTIONS

W hether growing indoors or out, mushroom cultivation can be a truly rewarding hobby that can provide you with a deep sense of self satisfaction. However, along your journey you will notice there are many obstacles that can make this great hobby challenging at times. There are some common mistakes that both novice and experienced growers alike can often make. Below I have outlined 8 of the most common problems as well as their solutions, in the case that you encounter them.

Problem: Lack of Moisture

As we have touched on several times throughout this book, mycelium needs moisture in order to develop a network and therefore eventually fruit mushrooms.

Moisture is also vitally important for improved temperature control of the substrate and better nutrient flow between your substrate and the mycelium.

Solution: Throughout the growing cycle pay close attention to the humidity and moisture levels. Make sure during the fruiting period that your mushrooms are watered daily using a spraying or misting device. The substrate should feel slightly damp without feeling too boggy. A good way to keep track of this is by using a hygrometer if that's something you want to invest in. 80-90% moisture content is ideal for most mushroom varieties.

Problem: Too Much Moisture

You have to strike a fine balance between keeping your mushrooms sufficiently hydrated and over-watering them. Too much moisture can lead to your substrate becoming soggy which becomes a breeding ground for mushrooms biggest competitors, mold and bacteria. You want to avoid seeing any puddles of water forming as this is a sure way to encourage contamination and reduced yield of mushrooms.

Solution: Don't overwater your substrate, and simply make sure there are no visible puddles. You can also poke holes in the bottom of your grow buckets or bags to allow the water to drain out of the bottom, or check your hygrometer and make sure that humidity is not going over 90%.

Problem: Contamination

By now the importance of keeping a good clean, sterile environment should be well understood. Contamination can creep in at any stage of the process, however is most likely to occur when making your own spawn. As soon as contamination is seen in your substrate, then unfortunately you will need to start again. Ensure you understand the different signs of contamination so you can easily differentiate your mycelium and contaminants.

Solution: Rushing your method is a common reason why contamination may occur, so be sure to follow the step by step guides so you are reducing the chance of contamination at each stage. Ensure to take the obvious steps seriously such as washing your hands, thoroughly cleaning down the surfaces, etc. Also, don't panic if you do get contamination in your substrate, it happens to all cultivators no matter how experienced they are. Learn from it and improve upon it.

Problem: Lack of Air Exchange

Mushrooms require regular exchange of fresh air because without it, carbon dioxide levels would build up (remember that mushrooms expel carbon dioxide when they breathe). If carbon dioxide levels are too high it can lead to stunted growth and reduced yield.

Solution: Regular fanning of your fruiting block is recommended on a daily basis. You can either do this with a fan, with the lid of your growing container or with any other instrument that can be used as such. Ensure there are enough holes cut into your grow bags if you are using them and if you are using a closed container then open it a couple of times a day to fan.

Problem: Substrate Not Tightly Packed Enough

This is one problem that I see all the time with novice growers. They will fill their grow bags or plastic containers with their substrate but not pack it down to a tight fit. Packing it tightly provides a much easier growing surface for the mycelium to operate as they are more easily able to make its way throughout the substrate.

Solution: This is fairly obvious–just make sure you pack down your substrate well as hard as you can.

Problem: Mycelium is Growing but Fails to Fruit

Occasionally you will find that you have been able to produce a lovely looking fruiting block which has been colonised with mycelium but that it fails to fruit. The most common reason for this would be a lack of moisture in the substrate as we have touched on previously. However, it could also be a result of a bad spawn, or a matter of the substrate and mycelium being poorly matched, not allowing the mycelium to get the energy required in order to fruit.

Solution: Ensure your mushrooms have adequate moisture content. If that does not seem to be the reason why they are not fruiting, change the supply of mycelium spawn for your next grow. Finally, double check that you have matched the mycelium to the preferred substrate.

Problem: Lack of Patience

Arguably the best skill to learn when cultivating mushrooms is that of patience. It can take time for mushrooms to go from spores to spawn to mushroom. People will often try to rush a particular stage as they get carried away with the excitement of wanting their block to fruit. Rushing any stage along the journey of growing mushrooms, unfortunately will only leave you disappointed. For example, if you transfer your agar to the grain, even if there are signs of contamination inside the dish just because it requires effort to make an agar transfer, then you should expect your grain spawn to become contaminated. Likewise, if you are desperate to get your substrate block outside and fruiting but it hasn't fully colonized yet, then expect a lower yield.

Solution: Follow the timescales and step by step methods in this book as a rough guide to when you should move on to each stage for each mushroom. However, most importantly you need to understand the life cycle of a mushroom so you are aware and understand why you are moving onto the next stage. This will help you immensely on your journey.

Problem: Deformities

If your mushrooms are not being produced to the high aesthetic standards you are familiar with then there will be an underlying reason for this. It will most likely be down to one of 3 reasons; inadequate lighting, poor airflow, or inadequate moisture levels.

Solution: First, make sure there is adequate lighting for your mushrooms. You could try installing an LED light as that has been shown in some studies to provide greater benefit to growth than indirect sunlight. This is not essential but could be worth trying. Make sure you have good airflow and the moisture levels are kept under control as previously discussed.

AFTERWORD

You've made it to the end! Congrats! I know that was a ton of information to soak up, but over time, you'll become more and more familiar with all the processes. Mushroom cultivation is a hobby that is increasing in popularity and understandably so. I speak from experience when I say that growing mushrooms is a truly rewarding and satisfying project that is difficult to stay away from once you've immersed yourself in it. Whether you are a novice who can't wait to get started, or an experienced grower who might learn a tip here or there to improve your overall growing experience, I hope that this book has provided you with value in some way.

After reading this book, you should have a thorough understanding of mushroom basics (i.e. the anatomy of a mushroom and its lifecycle), the cultivation process, and a general idea of commonly grown mushroom varieties and their preferred growing parameters. The step by step guides put together in this book were included to help your mushroom-growing experience run as smoothly as possible. So get out there and take the knowledge you have learned, apply it, and do it again and again until it becomes second nature. Some more advanced techniques have been covered such as how to generate your own spawn from a spore print and how to perform mushroom cloning, which I hope you have understood and are able to implement. I hope you're now inspired to take action and start growing, if you haven't already.

There are a few other great resources out there for some further reading, most notably Paul Stamets' book 'Growing Gourmet and Medicinal Mushrooms.' If you haven't already read it then it's definitely worth a read. It's a textbook-like publication for growing mushrooms that goes into much more detail for advanced growers.

I really hope you have enjoyed reading this book and I hope it lays the foundations of your mushroom cultivation journey. I have thoroughly enjoyed putting it together over the last year and would love for as many people as possible to use and benefit from it.

If you have truly enjoyed it and found it valuable, it would be greatly appreciated if you could head over to

Amazon and leave a review, as this really helps self-published authors like myself be seen! Reader feedback lets me know how I've done and what I can improve upon to serve you all in my next book. If you could head over to Amazon and leave a review that would be greatly appreciated.

Mush Love, everyone!

Kris Rowsan

KRowsan

P.S. I am currently working on another mushroom related book, and I can't wait for you to read it!

NOTES

DID YOU KNOW?

1. Zhang, M., Huang, J., Xie, X., & Holman, C. D. (2009). Dietary intakes of mushrooms and green tea combine to reduce the risk of breast cancer in Chinese women. International journal of cancer, 124(6), 1404–1408. https://doi.org/10.1002/ijc.24047

1. GET TO KNOW ME–I'M A FUNGI!

1. Zhong, L., Yan, P., Lam, W. C., Yao, L., & Bian, Z. (2019). *Coriolus Versicolor and Ganoderma Lucidum Related Natural Products as an Adjunct Therapy for Cancers: A Systematic Review and Meta-Analysis of Randomized Controlled Trials.* PubMed. https://pubmed.ncbi.nlm.nih.gov/31333449/
2. Tang, W., Gao, Y., Chen, G., Gao, H., Dai, X., Ye, J., Chan, E., Huang, M., & Zhou, S. (2005). A randomized, double-blind and placebo-controlled study of a Ganoderma lucidum polysaccharide extract in neurasthenia. *Journal of medicinal food*, 8(1), 53–58. https://doi.org/10.1089/jmf.2005.8.53
3. Mori, K., Inatomi, S., Ouchi, K., Azumi, Y., & Tuchida, T. (2009). Improving effects of the mushroom Yamabushitake (Hericium erinaceus) on mild cognitive impairment: a double-blind placebo-controlled clinical trial. *Phytotherapy research : PTR*, 23(3), 367–372. https://doi.org/10.1002/ptr.2634
4. Adenipekun, C.O & Lawal, Rasheedah. (2012). Uses of mushrooms in bioremediation: A Review. Biotechnology and Molecular Biology reviews. 7. 62-68. 10.5897/BMBR12.006.

Lightning Source UK Ltd.
Milton Keynes UK
UKHW012040110522
402858UK00002B/137

9 781919 648903